Project AIF

T0119580

DETERRENCE THEORY AND CHINESE BEHAVIOR

Abram N. Shulsky

Prepared for the United States Air Force
Approved for public release; distribution unlimited

RAND

China is emerging as a major global and regional player that will likely play a part in U.S. foreign policy well into the 21st century. A better understanding of China's interests, as well as its economic and military capabilities, will assist in crisis prevention and war avoidance. This report examines the applicability of deterrence theory to the future Sino-U.S relationship and examines the particular requirements that deterrence of China might impose.

This report is part of a larger project entitled "Chinese Defense Modernization and the USAF," which is being conducted in the Strategy and Doctrine Program of Project AIR FORCE under the sponsorship of the Deputy Chief of Staff for Air and Space Operations, U.S. Air Force (AF/XO), and the Commander, Pacific Air Forces (PACAF/CC). Comments may be directed to the author or to Zalmay Khalilzad, the program director.

PROJECT AIR FORCE

Project AIR FORCE, a division of RAND, is the Air Force federally funded research and development center (FFRDC) for studies and analysis. It provides the Air Force with independent analyses of policy alternatives affecting the development, employment, combat readiness, and support of current and future aerospace forces. Research is performed in four programs: Aerospace Force Development; Manpower, Personnel, and Training; Resource Management; and Strategy and Doctrine.

CONTENTS

> Managing the rise of China constitutes one of the most
> important challenges facing the United States in the early
> 21st century.
>
> —*Swaine and Tellis (2000), p. 1.*[1]

China's reforms since 1978 have given rise to unprecedented economic growth; if this course of development is sustained, China will be able to turn its great potential power, derived from its huge population, large territory, and significant natural resources, into actual power. The result could be, in the *very long term*, the rise of China as a rival to the United States as the world's predominant power.[2] However, long before that point is reached, if it ever is, China could become a significant rival in the East Asian region, one that might attempt to reduce and, ultimately, to expel U.S. forces and influence from that region.

In this context, the issue for U.S. policy is how to handle a rising power, a problem that predominant powers have faced many times throughout history. The current U.S. policy of engagement seeks to change the nature of, and, hence, the goals and objectives sought by, the Chinese regime: It seeks to make the Chinese regime more

---

[1] See this work for a discussion of the factors that will affect China's grand strategy as it seeks to develop its "comprehensive national power."

[2] Thompson (1988) discusses in detail the phenomenon of the rise and fall of predominant powers and the possibility that large-scale war will accompany the process.

democratic and more willing to cooperate with existing international norms in such areas as nonproliferation, respect for human rights, and free trade. According to the Department of Defense's strategy for the East Asia–Pacific region: "Prospects for peace and prosperity in Asia depend heavily upon China's role as a responsible member of the international community." (U.S. Department of Defense [DoD], 1988, p. 30.)

Regardless of how one assesses the likelihood that the current engagement policy will achieve its ultimate objective,[3] the question of how to avoid conflict in the meantime remains. While the engagement policy gives China's leaders an incentive to maintain good relations with the United States, that incentive may be overpowered by other considerations, such as concerns about territorial sovereignty (including Taiwan and the South China Sea) and the maintenance of Communist Party rule. Thus, it would be a mistake to conclude that the Chinese interest in economic and technological development makes a conflict with the United States impossible. Accordingly, it is of interest to consider how the United States might be able to deter China from using force in a manner inimical to U.S. interests.

The historical record contains many occasions on which the People's Republic of China (PRC) took military action contrary to important interests of the United States and the former Soviet Union. In many cases, one or the other tried to deter China but found this task rather difficult to accomplish, despite the vast disparity in military power between itself and the PRC. This report discusses the instances in which some element of deterrence might be thought to have been operative, although it is often unclear whether there was a conscious effort to deter.[4]

It is the contention of this report that the future Sino-U.S. context will illustrate many of the problems of deterrence theory that have been discussed in recent decades; deterrence theory will be, in general, more difficult to apply than it was in the U.S.-Soviet Cold War

---

[3]See Khalilzad et al. (1999), pp. 63–69, for a critique of engagement policy.

[4]The appendix discusses cases in which China was faced with the problem of an adversary taking, or being about to take, undesired actions; again, it is often unclear whether China was engaged in a deliberate attempt to deter.

context. A review of the deterrence literature suggests several areas of theoretical concerns that would be relevant to deterrence in a Sino-U.S context.

Since deterrence primarily relies on the *threat* of future harm, the deterrer's credibility is obviously a key factor in making deterrence work. Credibility may be determined by many factors; one of the most important is the importance to the deterrer of the stakes involved. In the Sino-U.S. context, the importance of the stakes involved in many of the potential deterrence situations may not be so clear.

In the most important case, the United States would wish to deter Chinese use of force against Taiwan. However, this would not necessarily involve any change in its "one China" policy, which implies that the U.S. interest is only in the means by which Taiwan and China might be unified. According to this policy, the United States is willing to accept the strategic consequences of Taiwan's incorporation into the PRC (e.g., that Taiwanese ports could become bases for the Chinese People's Liberation Army Navy). Thus, the United States would have to convince China that, despite its apparent unconcern with the *strategic substance* of reunification, its interest in the *process* is substantial enough to lead the United States to incur large costs. The Chinese leadership might not find such a distinction credible; thus, it might believe either that the United States would not fight or that its willingness to fight indicated a shift in U.S. policy toward actual support for Taiwanese independence. In the latter case, the Chinese might be difficult to deter because of a belief that the result of their forbearance might well be not a continuation of the status quo but rather an invigorated Taiwanese push for independence.

Closely related to the question of defining and measuring the stakes of the parties in a potential conflict is the question of assessing the strength of one side's "commitment" to achieving its goals, however understood. To a large extent, the strength of commitment reflects the importance of the stakes. However, the degree of commitment can be increased, either because of circumstances or as a result of deliberate manipulation of the value of the stake, giving the side whose commitment is thus strengthened a relative bargaining advantage.

The PRC leadership's discussion of the Taiwan issue under the rubric of protecting territorial integrity has the effect of increasing the value of the stakes; the leadership seeks to convince others that the irretrievable failure to gain control of a territory it has never ruled would constitute a humiliating defeat, which it would therefore be compelled to run great risks to avoid. However, in the past, the PRC leadership has been willing, for example, in the course of the rapprochement with the United States in 1971–1972, to shelve the Taiwan issue, seemingly indefinitely.[5] Thus, should the leadership decide at some time that it is was necessary to achieve reunification within a specific time (perhaps because the leadership came to think that time was not on its side and that the overall trend was toward *de jure* Taiwanese independence), it might have some difficulty establishing that it no longer possessed its earlier patience with respect to this issue. Domestic political considerations could also raise the importance of the Taiwan issue to an American administration. In both cases, the differences between the American and Chinese political systems might make it hard to gauge exactly how much domestic pressure the other side's leadership was under.

It is generally believed that the side defending the status quo has a certain advantage. With respect to the potentially most serious source of Sino-U.S. conflict—Taiwan—the status quo is complex and may be understood differently by the two sides. Taiwan is currently independent *de facto* but enjoys only limited sovereignty *de jure*. It has normal diplomatic relations with only a handful of states and none of them the world's major powers. Thus, the two sides may emphasize different aspects of the current situation, the United States focusing primarily on Taiwan's *de facto* independence and China on the nearly universal recognition of the "one China" principle and on Beijing's right to represent that China. If a future Chinese threat to Taiwan arose out of some action the latter took to acquire a degree of legal or diplomatic expression of its *de facto* independence,

---

[5]Kissinger (1979), p. 1062, quotes Mao as saying: "We can do without them [Taiwan] for the time being; and let it come after 100 years." While the reference to "100 years" was perhaps poetic license, the main point was clear: The Taiwan issue was not to be allowed to derail the Sino-U.S. rapprochement. Although Mao may have hoped that the shock of the eventual U.S. derecognition of the government of the Republic of China would itself lead to reunification on terms favorable to Beijing, he did not have any guarantee of this and did not insist on any.

each side could see itself as essentially defending the status quo and could believe that its deterrent threats gained credibility from that circumstance.

Deterrence typically seeks to clarify the actions by the adversary that are to be deterred, i.e., to specify the actions to which the deterrer will respond by inflicting some form of punishment on the aggressor. Thus, it may be harder to make clear and credible deterrent threats that cover all possible adversary actions that one wishes to prevent. As one study of the successes and failures of U.S. deterrence attempts concluded,

> *Nations interested in changing the status quo normally have more than one option for doing so.* . . . A deterrence policy which discourages an opponent from employing some options but not others is incomplete and may not prevent a failure of deterrence. An opponent who is bent upon altering a given status quo may design around the viable aspects of the deterrence strategy that confronts him. (George and Smoke, 1974, pp. 520–521; emphasis in the original.)

China has, in the past, often been adept at calibrating its actions in such a manner as to avoid a strong response from its adversary.

To deter an adversary, one must possess not only credibility but also military capability. The United States retains sufficient strategic nuclear strength that its ability to do unacceptable damage to China cannot be questioned. But assessments of relative conventional military capabilities, such as would be relevant to judge one side's ability to carry out threatened military actions, are more difficult; the actual use of military forces always carries with it the possibility of unforeseen occurrences. Although overall U.S. military power vastly exceeds that of China, and will continue to do so during the first decades of the 21st century, the Chinese might believe that a surprise attack by large numbers of missiles might be able to inflict serious damage on U.S. power-projection capabilities, thereby producing a serious psychological shock that would hamper further U.S. action. Even if this were a miscalculation on their part, the result could be that, contrary to U.S. expectations, the Chinese would not be deterred by the presence of a powerful U.S. force in their vicinity, any

xii   Deterrence Theory and Chinese Behavior

more than the Japanese were deterred by the forward deployment of the U.S. Pacific Fleet at Pearl Harbor.

Politically, the deterrent value of U.S. military superiority might be diminished by a Chinese belief that various political constraints will inhibit the ability of the United States to use it. For example, the Chinese may believe that U.S. sensitivity to casualties will limit U.S. military actions. Hence, the Chinese perception of usable U.S. military strength may be very different from what the United States might believe.

In any case, deterrence rests not so much on the deterrer's will and ability to use military force as on its adversary's perceptions of them. These perceptions are determined not only by the objective realities as a neutral, dispassionate observer might determine them but also by a whole host of cultural factors. For example, the United States often believes that a crisis deployment sends a strong signal of its willingness to use force and thus expects it to have a strong deterrent effect. However, to a country, such as China, whose strategic tradition emphasizes the importance of surprise attacks, the deliberate parading of forces might seem more like an alternative to their use; after all, if the adversary had intended to attack, it would have been more discreet about its preparations to do so. Similarly, the United States might see the absence of visible preparations for the use of force (which were displayed precisely to exercise a deterrent effect) as a sign that its adversary lacks the will or the capability; instead, it might reflect the adversary's desire to achieve surprise when it did in fact attack.

Successful deterrence of China has often required the threat of very high levels of violence or a serious threat to the regime's internal stability or control of the country. In the future, given the probable nature of the stakes in a likely Sino-U.S. conflict, it is unclear whether the United States will be willing or able to make these types of threats, especially nuclear threats. Thus, the main problem to be addressed is that of deterring the Chinese from using force in cases in which threats of massive retaliation may not be credible.

The Chinese have often shown a willingness to resort to force precisely because they see the resulting tension as being in their interest. The purpose of the tension may be domestic mobilization or may be intended to exert a psychological impact on a foreign power and hence bring about a change in its policies. This type of behavior may be difficult to deter. Threats to use (limited amounts of) force in reply may indeed play into a Chinese strategy of increasing tension. The key element here seems to be China's confidence that it can control the level of tension and the risk of escalation, rather than avoid them altogether. Hence, a strategy of carefully controlled escalatory threats and actions may be an inappropriate means of achieving a deterrent effect, since it does nothing to shake that confidence.

Deterrence theory assumes a certain transparency of intent and capability. In principle, the party to be deterred should be able to calculate the deterrer's willingness to use force and capability to do so with some degree of accuracy, to determine whether or not the deteree should proceed with its desired course of action. In fact, in many historical cases, the reality was quite different; the motives of the parties were opaque, and the strength of their military capabilities was misestimated, often wildly so.

Unless Sino-U.S. relations deteriorate to Cold War–like levels, it would seem that nuclear deterrence will have little role to play in handling the types of conflict scenarios that might arise. This poses a difficult but not insurmountable challenge to U.S. policymakers. The key may be to seek nonmilitary means of deterrence, i.e., diplomatic ways to manipulate the tension to China's disadvantage. For example, in future crises, China will have to be concerned that its threat or use of force will encourage neighboring states to see her as an emerging strategic threat against which they must band together. This type of regional reaction, encouraged and supported by the United States, may be the best deterrent to Chinese use of force in the region.

ACKNOWLEDGMENTS

The author wishes to thank the project's action officers, Majors Mark Stokes, Stephen Cunico, and Milton Johnson of the Directorate of Operations, Headquarters, U.S. Air Force, and Major Rod Erikson and James Hertsch of the National Air Intelligence Center for their help and encouragement. He also wishes to thank his colleagues at RAND for their criticism and suggestions and, in particular, Luetta Pope and Grace Young, for their able secretarial assistance. Phyllis Gilmore edited the manuscript with her usual skill and good humor.

The author is grateful for the helpful and frank comments of Jonathan Pollack and of Arthur Waldron of the University of Pennsylvania, who reviewed earlier drafts of this report.

ABBREVIATIONS

CPV	Chinese People's Volunteers (PRC troops in the Korean War)
DoD	U.S. Department of Defense
DPP	Democratic Progressive Party (of the ROC)
FBIS	Foreign Broadcast Information Service
GMT	Greenwich Mean Time
KMT	Kuomintang (Nationalist Party, ROC)
NATO	North Atlantic Treaty Organization
PLA	People's Liberation Army (PRC)
POW	Prisoner of war
PRC	People's Republic of China
ROC	Republic of China (Taiwan)
SEATO	Southeast Asia Treaty Organization
UN	United Nations
USSR	Union of Soviet Socialist Republics

Chapter One

INTRODUCTION

As China modernizes its military capabilities, it will seek to play a more active political-military role in the affairs of East Asia. At the same time, U.S. policy calls for the maintenance of strong military forces in the region that "promote security and stability, deter conflict, give substance to [its] security commitments and ensure [its] continued access to the region." (U.S. Department of Defense [DoD], 1998, p. 9.) The confluence of these two tendencies raises the possibility of potential military conflict between the two countries; at the political level, it poses the question of how "rules of the game" can be established to reduce the risk of military conflict.

This report examines one aspect of this question, the role of deterrence in U.S. policy toward China. As discussed in Chapter Two, deterrence can only be one facet of overall U.S. policy, since the basic issue is that of managing the emergence of a potential new great power into the global arena. This clearly involves much more than deterrence of specific Chinese actions; nevertheless, deterrence is of special importance for the U.S. armed forces, including the U.S. Air Force. Chapter Three examines the historical record of attempts the United States and the former Soviet Union have made to deter certain Chinese actions; the record is decidedly mixed. Given how much weaker China was than either of these two adversaries, what stands out is how difficult the deterrence problem was for them.

Chapter Four examines the role deterrence can play in Sino-U.S. relations and attempts to explain what specific characteristics of that relationship are likely to affect the deterrence question. It addresses the question of the types of Chinese actions that the United States is likely to wish to deter.[1] This sets the stage for Chapter Five, which looks at the relevant characteristics of Sino-U.S. relations in the light of deterrence theory.   In general, many of the difficulties and perplexities of deterrence that have been discussed at the theoretical level are reflected in the particulars of the Sino-U.S. relationship. The report concludes (in Chapter Six) with some reflections on the problem of deterring China in the future, including a more detailed discussion of issues involving the possible requirement to deter Chinese use of force against Taiwan.

The appendix looks at the historical record of Chinese behavior directed against adversaries who were potentially engaged in actions detrimental to China; in many cases, the Chinese may not have deliberately intended to deter their adversaries (rather than, say, to "punish" them) but took action in situations to which Western observers would typically apply deterrence theory.

---

[1]This report was completed before the period of heightened tension surrounding the Taiwanese presidential election of March 18, 2000.

Chapter Two

THE ROLE OF DETERRENCE IN U.S. CHINA POLICY

> Managing the rise of China constitutes one of the most important challenges facing the United States in the early 21st century.
>
> —*Swaine and Tellis (2000), p. 1.*[1]

China's reforms since 1978 have given rise to unprecedented economic growth; if this course of development is sustained, China will be able to turn its great potential power, derived from its huge population, large territory, and significant natural resources, into actual power. The result could be, in the *very long term*, the rise of China as a rival to the United States as the world's predominant power.[2] However, long before that point is reached, if it ever is, China could become a significant rival in the East Asian region, one that might attempt to reduce and, ultimately, to expel U.S. forces and influence from that region.

In this context, the issue for U.S. policy is how to handle a rising power, a problem that predominant powers have faced many times throughout history. The various possible fundamental policy directions that predominant powers have pursued are well known: preemption, containment, balancing, and accommodation (or

---

[1]See this work for a discussion of the factors that will affect China's grand strategy as it seeks to develop its "comprehensive national power."

[2]Thompson (1988) discusses in detail the phenomenon of the rise and fall of predominant powers and the possibility that large-scale war will accompany the process.

appeasement). These policies are all understandable within the realist tradition, which sees other powers as having essentially fixed goals and objectives (such as security, prosperity, and the enhancement of their own influence and power within the international system).[3] The current U.S. policy of engagement, by contrast, is more ambitious than these "realist" strategies in that it seeks to change the nature of, and, hence, the goals and objectives sought by, the Chinese regime: It seeks to make the Chinese regime more democratic and more willing to cooperate with existing international norms in such areas as nonproliferation, respect for human rights, and free trade. Ultimately, it aims at inducing China to adjust to current international norms to such an extent that its increase in political-military power and influence will have minimal effects on the rest of the world. According to DoD's strategy for the East Asia–Pacific region: "Prospects for peace and prosperity in Asia depend heavily upon China's role as a responsible member of the international community." (DoD, 1998, p. 30.)

Regardless of how one assesses the likelihood that the current engagement policy will achieve its ultimate objective,[4] the question remains of how to avoid conflict in the meantime. The engagement policy, or any policy that similarly provides important benefits to China, gives its leaders an incentive to maintain good relations with the United States.[5] That incentive, however, may be overpowered by other considerations, such as concerns about territorial sovereignty (including Taiwan and the South China Sea) and the maintenance of

---

[3]Robert Gilpin emphasizes the importance of the "rules of the game" and the struggle among nations to influence them:

> Thus the study of international political change must focus on the international system and especially on the efforts of political actors to change the international system in order to advance their own interests. Whether these interests are security, economic gain, or ideological goals, the achievement of state objectives is dependent on the nature of the international system (i.e., the governance of the system, the rules of the system, the recognition of rights, etc.). As is the case in any social or political system, the process of international political change ultimately reflects the efforts of individuals or groups to transform institutions and systems in order to advance their interests. (Gilpin, 1983, p. 10.)

[4]See Khalilzad et al. (1999), pp. 63–69, for a critique of engagement policy.

[5]Examples of benefits would be access to U.S. markets, investment capital, and technology—all of which are important, if not crucial, for the attainment of what the Chinese refer to as "comprehensive national power." See Khalilzad (1999), pp. 3–16, for a discussion of these conflicting motivations of Chinese policymakers.

Communist Party rule. In addition, Chinese dissatisfaction with U.S. preeminence in the world (as highlighted, for example, by Chinese opposition to the U.S. role in leading the intervention of the North Atlantic Treaty Organization [NATO] in Kosovo) also tends to counteract the Chinese desire to maintain good relations with the United States.

Thus, Chinese interest in economic and technological development does not make a conflict with the United States impossible. Accordingly, it is of interest to consider how the United States might be able to deter China from using force in a manner inimical to U.S. interests. It must be remembered, however, that this discussion should not be taken as meaning that considerations of "immediate deterrence" will, or should, dominate the Sino-U.S. relationship.[6] As noted, the more fundamental issue involves the integration of a rising China into the international system; occasions may arise in which deterrence would be an important and perhaps even necessary part of that process, but it can only be a part and, hopefully, a small part at that.

---

[6]I use "immediate deterrence" in the sense of Morgan (1983), p. 30, who defines it as "the relationship between opposing states where at least one side is seriously considering an attack while the other is mounting a threat of retaliation in order to prevent it" and contrasts it with "general deterrence," which "relates to opponents who maintain armed forces to regulate their relationship even though neither is anywhere near mounting an attack." In the latter sense, a deterrence relationship between major powers with important opposing interests would seem to be all but inevitable.

Chapter Three

THE HISTORICAL RECORD

The People's Republic of China (PRC) has taken action contrary to important interests of the United States and the former Soviet Union on many occasions. In many case, one or the other tried to deter China but found this task rather difficult to accomplish, despite the vast disparity in military power between itself and the PRC. In other cases, there was no attempt at immediate deterrence, but there was an element of general deterrence.[1] This chapter briefly discusses the instances in which immediate deterrence was attempted or in which some element of general deterrence (i.e., some effect arising from the military posture of China's adversary) might be thought to have been operative.

U.S. DETERRENCE OF CHINA

"Neutralization" of the Taiwan Strait (1950)

One of President Harry S. Truman's first acts in response to the North Korean invasion of the south was to interpose the Seventh Fleet between the Communist PRC on the mainland and the Nationalist (Kuomintang [KMT]) regime on Taiwan. Although this was presented as a "neutralization" of the Taiwan Strait, i.e., as designed to prevent either party from attacking the other, it in effect served to prevent the Communists from completing their victory in the civil war. Since a successful attack on Taiwan was so far beyond

---

[1]As Patrick Morgan (1983) describes these types of deterrence.

the PRC's capabilities that it was not even attempted, this can be considered a case of successful deterrence by denial.[2]

U.S. Fails to Deter Chinese Entry into Korea (1950)

In terms of its consequences, the greatest U.S. policy failure with respect to China was its failure to deter the Chinese entrance into the Korean War in 1950. Once U.S. and United Nations (UN) troops crossed the 38th parallel,[3] the United States relied primarily on assurances rather than threats to keep the Chinese out of the war: The United States tried to assure China that it would not attack Chinese territory, that it would not destroy Chinese hydroelectric power plants on the Yalu River, and so forth.[4] These assurances probably fell wide of the mark because they did not address the fundamental Chinese fear, which was that the U.S. actions in Korea inevitably threatened China.[5]

But it is not clear that a more forceful deterrent strategy would have been successful either.[6] As noted, it appears that Mao believed that

-----

[2]As one Chinese observer noted,

> Before June 27 [1950], the problem of liberating Taiwan pitted the strength of the PLA [People's Liberation Army] against the Chiang Kai-shek remnants, with the help of the American imperialists occupying a background position. Since June 27, the problem of liberating Taiwan pits the strength of the PLA against the American imperialists, with the Kuomintang bandit remnants moving into the background.

World Culture, Vol. XXII, No. 1, July 7, 1950, unsigned question-and-answer section, p. 23, as cited in Whiting (1960), p. 63. On p. 64, Whiting goes on to note that

> [t]his analysis tacitly argued for postponing the Taiwan invasion until after Pyongyang had forced the United States out of Korea. By implication, the analysis conceded the futility of attacking Taiwan as long as the threat of American interdiction remained.

[3]The fact that the U.S.-UN forces did cross the 38th parallel, the pre-1950 dividing line between North and South Korea, itself could be seen as a failure of Chinese deterrence efforts. See the appendix.

[4]Tsou (1963), p. 583, lists the various steps taken in this regard; according to Tsou, U.S. policy assumed that "the Chinese Communists would be willing to negotiate on the basis of a buffer zone and access to power supply in North Korea. . . . [This] turned out to be false."

[5]See Christensen (1996), Ch. 5, and Tsou (1963), pp. 576–577. Tsou believes that, consonant with their "grim, ideologically colored view of American intentions," the Chinese thought that U.S. actions in Korea demonstrated that it was following in Japan's footsteps.

[6]Whiting (1960), pp. 97–98, quotes from a speech President Truman gave on September 1, 1950, that could be read as a threat to broaden the war to China if

U.S. actions in Korea—together with the deployment, in response to outbreak of the Korean War, of the Seventh Fleet to "neutralize" the Taiwan Strait—presaged an attack on China. Hence, threats to bomb Chinese cities or industry probably would not have been an adequate deterrent, since, from Mao's perspective, such dangers would have to be faced in any case. Mao could well have believed that it was in China's interest to precipitate the war in 1950, when the United States was still fighting in Korea, rather than to wait and allow the United States to prepare its attack on China at its own pace.

This illustrates the important theoretical point, sometimes overlooked, that threats alone do not deter a country from taking an action. Logically, there must be a concomitant reassurance (which may typically be implicit rather than explicit) that, if the action to be deterred is not taken, the threats will not be carried out. In this case, that reassurance may have been impossible (at least after the use of U.S. naval power to protect Taiwan): Mao would have believed that the threats (e.g., bombing of China's cities and industry) would likely have been carried out in any case; hence, their deterrent value was essentially nil.

Shelling of Jinmen (Quemoy) and Mazu (Matsu) (1954 and 1958)[7]

Although the onset of the shelling of Jinmen and Mazu in 1954 and again in 1958 did not take the United States entirely by surprise, in neither case can the United States be said to have tried to deter the initial shelling of the offshore islands. However, once the 1954 crisis began, the United States faced the question of whether the Chinese posed a serious threat to invade the islands, either as an isolated engagement or as a prelude to an invasion of Taiwan.

The U.S. commitment to the defense of the offshore islands was ambiguous. Public statements of support for the defense of Taiwan

---

Chinese troops intervened in Korea, although, as he notes, its ostensible purpose "was to reassure Peking on U.S. intentions," i.e., to disclaim any intention of attacking China. However, as noted in the text, there was little likelihood that such reassurances would be effective.

[7]The circumstances of the 1954–1955 crisis are discussed in greater detail in the appendix.

never specified whether Jinmen and Mazu were included, to say nothing of the more remote Dachen island group. (Zhang, 1992, p. 210.) The mutual security treaty signed with Taiwan on December 5, 1954, covered Taiwan and the Pescadores "and such other territories as may be determined by the mutual agreement."

Following the Chinese seizure of Yijiangshan island in mid-January 1955, Congress, by means of the Formosa Resolution, authorized President Dwight D. Eisenhower to use force to defend the offshore islands when the president judged their defense to be required or expedient in assuring the defense of Taiwan. While the formula retained some ambiguity, the Chinese saw this as an American commitment to the defense of the offshore islands. (Zhang, 1992, p. 220.) In the following months, U.S. spokesmen made references to U.S. nuclear weapons in the context of the Taiwan Strait crisis.[8] Having occupied the Dachen islands in February (after the Taiwanese troops stationed there evacuated them), the Chinese were faced with the question of whether to attempt to seize Jinmen and Mazu as well. Observing a clearer U.S. commitment to the islands, backed up by the brandishing of nuclear weapons, the Chinese chose to wind down the crisis. In April, Zhou Enlai announced that

> the Chinese people do not want a war with the United States. The Chinese government is willing to sit down with the U.S. government to discuss the question of relaxing tensions in the Far East, and especially the question of decreasing tensions in the Taiwan area.[9]

In the 1958 crisis, the U.S. commitment to the defense of the offshore islands—which was not forthcoming until several weeks after the onset of the crisis[10]—did not suffice to deter a continuing Chinese

---

[8]For example, President Eisenhower, when asked at a press conference on March 16, 1955, whether the United States would "use tactical atomic weapons in a general war in Asia" responded that, "[a]gainst a strictly military target . . . the answer would be 'yes.'" Eisenhower "hoped this answer would have some effect in persuading the Chinese Communists of the strength of our determination." (Eisenhower, 1963, p. 477.)

[9]Premier Zhou's Announcement at Bandung [Conference of Nonaligned Nations] on April 23, 1955, *Renmin Ribao*, April 24, 1955, p. 1, cited in Zhang (1992), p. 222.

[10]The shelling began on August 23, 1958; the first public statement committing the United States to the defense of the islands was made on September 4 by then–Secretary of State John Foster Dulles.

bombardment of Jinmen. The bombardment threatened to cut off efforts to resupply the garrison there; unbroken, this artillery blockade would have ultimately required Taiwan to abandon the island. China may have calculated that the blockade could not be lifted unless the United States used air power to attack artillery sites and other targets on the mainland and that the United States would be unwilling to expand the conflict in that manner.[11] In the event, U.S. naval assistance to the Taiwanese was sufficient to enable them to resupply their troops, thus obviating any need to attack sites on the mainland.

1996 Missile Exercise Against Taiwan

The United States did not attempt to deter China from conducting missile and other military exercises against Taiwan in 1996. However, sending two carrier battle groups helped diminish the psychological effect of the Chinese exercises. Whether this action should be seen as a deterrent depends on whether there was any fear that further Chinese military action—e.g., more serious harassment or an outright invasion—was a likely possibility. Assuming that it was not, the U.S. action does not appear to be a case of deterrence.[12]

SOVIET DETERRENCE OF CHINA

USSR Deters Further Chinese Attacks on the Sino-Soviet Border (1969)

The Chinese decided to raise tensions on their border with the Soviet Union in 1969, leading to a major clash on March 2 on the disputed island of Zhenbao (Damanskiy) in the Ussuri River.[13] The Chinese evidently wanted to preempt any Soviet attempt to put pressure on

---

[11]See George and Smoke (1974), pp. 365–366, for this interpretation. For an alternative explanation of Chinese motives in the 1958 crisis, see Christensen (1996), Ch. 6, who argues that Mao's primary purpose in raising tensions in the Taiwan Strait was to mobilize popular support for the Great Leap Forward.

[12]This paragraph deals only with the limited question of whether the United States deterred further Chinese military action against Taiwan. For the context and more detail concerning this episode, see the discussion in the appendix.

[13]This episode is discussed in greater detail in the appendix.

them; they may have felt that passivity on their part would only tempt the Soviets to see how much political leverage they could extract from their forces on the Sino-Soviet border, which had been built up during the second half of the 1960s. The immediate cause of the Chinese decision was probably the Soviet invasion of Czechoslovakia in August 1968, which emphasized the potential danger the Soviet buildup posed and which probably heightened the need the Chinese perceived to show that they could not be bullied. (Gelman, 1982, pp. 28–29.)[14]

The Soviets now faced the possibility of a continuing low-level conflict along the border, as the Chinese tried to promote their territorial claims. The Soviets sought to avoid this prospect by opening talks with the Chinese but were rebuffed, at times in a humiliating manner.[15]

The Soviets thus had the problem of deterring the Chinese from conducting a series of provocation actions. This situation may have seemed particularly frustrating and baffling to the Soviets, since China appeared to be disregarding what would seem to be the manifest Soviet advantage in both conventional and nuclear forces. As one study summarized, "A central aim of Soviet policy from March through September 1969 was therefore to create credibility for the threat to escalate, through a combination of means." (Gelman, 1982, p. 34.)

The Soviets eventually succeeded in bringing the Chinese to the table by escalating the conflict. On March 15, the Soviets took the initiative in causing a larger firefight on the same island. (Wich, 1980,

---

[14]See Wich (1980) for a somewhat more elaborate interpretation, according to which the Chinese were mainly interested in demonstrating to other ruling Communist parties, primarily those of North Korea and North Vietnam, the "social imperialist" nature of Soviet policy by creating a situation in which the Soviet Union would be induced to use force against China.

[15]Wich (1980) notes on p. 117 that

> [at the Ninth Chinese Communist Party Congress in April 1969 Chinese Defense Minister] Lin [Biao] disclosed that Premier Kosygin on 21 March had asked to communicate with the Chinese leadership by telephone—one of a long series of attempts by Moscow to remove the burden of the border conflict—but that the Chinese on the next day replied with a memorandum indicating that, in the view of the present state of relations, it was "unsuitable" to communicate by telephone and the Soviets would have to conduct their business through diplomatic channels.

p. 113.) Later in the year, they instigated conflicts on their border with Xinjiang (Kissinger, 1979, p. 177[16]), an area of political sensitivity for the Chinese because of prior instances there of Uighur nationalism. Indeed, the Soviets deliberately referred in their own publications to separatist tendencies in Xinjiang, suggesting that they might provide support to antigovernment groups as a way of putting pressure on Beijing.[17] The Soviets also dredged up a former Chinese general of Uighur nationality; he wrote an article in July 1969 entitled "Maoist Outrages on Uigur [sic] Soil," in which he recalled his participation, from 1944 to 1949, in the establishment of the separatist (and Soviet-influenced) East Turkestan Republic. (Taipov (1969.)[18]

In addition, Soviet media also pointedly recalled three occasions on which the Soviet Union had fought large-scale battles in the Far East: in 1929, against local "Chinese militarists" in Manchuria; in 1939, against the Japanese at Khalkin-Gol; and in 1945, when the Soviets ousted the Japanese from Manchuria.[19] More ominously, the Soviets also brandished an implicit nuclear threat against China during this period. According to Henry Kissinger,

> On August 18 [1969] a middle-level State Department specialist in Soviet affairs, William Stearman, was having lunch with a Soviet Embassy official when, out of the blue, the Russian asked what the U.S. reaction would be to a Soviet attack on Chinese nuclear facilities. (Kissinger, 1979, p. 183.)

---

[16]Kissinger bases his belief that the Soviets instigated these incidents on the Soviet logistics advantage given their location:

> [W]hen I looked at a detailed map and saw that the Sinkiang incidents took place only a few miles from the Soviet railhead and several hundred miles from any Chinese railhead, it occurred to me that Chinese military leaders would not have picked such an unpropitious spot to attack.

However, the political context as described in the text seems to provide an equally, if not more, convincing argument.

[17]For example, Mirov (1969), referenced in Wich (1980), p. 172, claimed that some residents of Xinjiang wished to rename the area "Uighurstan."

[18]According to Gelman (1982), the rebellion that produced the East Turkestan Republic was "orchestrated by the USSR."

[19]See Gelman (1982), pp. 36–37, for the citations to the Soviet media; in some cases, the Soviets explicitly pointed out the lesson that they wished China to draw from these historical examples.

Also during August, a *Pravda* editorial referred to China's nuclear potential as a matter of concern not only for the Soviet Union but for the international community as well, perhaps suggesting the justifiability of a preemptive strike.[20] The editorial mentioned the dangers created by "the armaments, lethal weapons, and modern means of delivery that now exist"; it is no coincidence (as the Soviets would say) that August also saw the appointment of a Strategic Rocket Forces general as the new commander of the Soviet Far Eastern Military District. (Hinton, 1971, pp. 52–53.)

Finally, in September 1969, the Chinese agreed to negotiations, inviting Soviet Premier Kosygin to stop in Beijing on his return home from Ho Chi Minh's funeral in Hanoi. A Chinese government statement of October 7 argued that the "struggle of principle" with the Soviet Union could continue for a long time yet would not make normal state-to-state relations impossible. (Wich, 1980, p. 209.) Thus, the Chinese were finally forced to give up the use of border incidents as a means of conducting their anti-Soviet policy. In this sense, then, the Soviet escalation following the March 2 incident may be seen as a successful instance of deterrence. However, it is worth remembering that Soviet "deterrence" did not affect the main issue that lay behind the border incidents, i.e., the Chinese shift from the isolation of the Cultural Revolution to semialliance with the United States.

USSR Fails to Deter Chinese Attack on Vietnam (1979)[21]

The Soviet Union and Vietnam signed a treaty on November 3, 1978, in accordance with which the two parties promised to "consult" in case one of them was attacked or threatened with attack, for the purpose of "eliminating the threat and taking appropriate and effective measures to safeguard peace and security in their countries."[22] Although Foreign Minister Andrei Gromyko emphasized this provi-

---

[20]"The Adventurist Course of Peking" (1969).

[21]This section draws heavily on Gelman (1982), pp. 91–102. See the appendix for a more detailed discussion of the Chinese invasion of Vietnam.

[22]As Gelman (1982), p. 91, notes, the Soviet commitment under this treaty was weaker than its comparable treaty commitment to other Communist states, which was to provide immediate military aid in the event of attack.

sion in early December in the course of the treaty ratification proceedings, the Soviets did not try, during the following months, to use it to deter the Chinese from invading Vietnam. Neither did the Soviets warn China of any military action in case it invaded Vietnam.

There is some evidence that the Soviet Union thought that Chinese preparations for the invasion represented merely a form of pressure on Vietnam; the Soviets tended to play down the reports of Chinese military concentrations and to treat them as attempts at political intimidation. If so, they might have thought that focusing attention on the Chinese threat, and the concomitant creation of a crisis atmosphere, would only play into Chinese hands.

When it actually occurred, the Chinese invasion of Vietnam was not an impressive operation militarily: It proceeded only slowly and at great cost. In addition, the Chinese were very explicit about the limited nature of their military goals and, having achieved them, withdrew unilaterally. Thus, the costs to Vietnam were relatively small, and the Soviet Union was never forced to make the difficult decision of whether or not to aid Vietnam militarily.

In this case, the Soviets may have misread Chinese intentions, thinking that the mere existence of large Soviet forces on its northern border would serve as a deterrent even in the absence of specific threats or warnings. In addition, the Soviets may have refrained from committing themselves too explicitly to the defense of Vietnam precisely because they did not wish to run the risk of war with China. However, if the Chinese had been more ambitious and more successful militarily, the Soviets would have found themselves in a difficult situation, forced either to attack China or to suffer a major loss of credibility.

Thus, while the Soviets failed to prevent the Chinese invasion of Vietnam, the implicit threat that their Brezhnev-era Far Eastern military buildup conveyed may have induced the Chinese to limit their military action to a level that the Soviets could ignore without loss of prestige.

Chapter Four

DETERRENCE IN THE CONTEXT OF SINO-U.S. RELATIONS

Although *deterrence* may be simply defined as "the persuasion of one's opponent that the costs and/or risks of a given course of action he might take outweigh its benefits" (George and Smoke, 1974, p. 11), the development of the theory of deterrence was clearly influenced by its origins in the attempt to grapple with the devastating power of nuclear weapons at the beginning of the Cold War and by the difficulty, if not impossibility, of defending against a nuclear attack well enough to significantly reduce the harm it could inflict. The theory itself grew up in that environment, which shaped many of its specific features and the questions it addressed.

On the basis of the above definition, deterrence could be enhanced not only by increasing the costs and/or risks of the action to be deterred but also by reducing its expected benefits. Hence, the ability to defend a threatened territory (thereby reducing the benefits a potential aggressor could expect to gain from attacking it) is logically as much of a deterrent as the ability to inflict retaliatory damage on the aggressor's homeland. However, because of the historical circumstance noted above, deterrence theory has emphasized retaliating after an attack rather than defending the threatened territory well enough to deny the attacker the expected benefits of his action. Accordingly, some theorists have distinguished sharply between *deterrence* (which is seen as depending primarily on the threat of punishment, i.e., on increasing the prospective cost of the action to be deterred) and *defense* (which seeks to deny the party to be deterred any benefits from its contemplated action). However, it should be noted that, on the basis of the simple definition cited at the beginning of this chapter, the ability to mount an effective defense—thereby demonstrating the capability to deny the aggressor the prize that he seeks—can itself function as a deterrent.[1]

This ambiguity reflects the origins of deterrence theory in the novel problem that the Soviet acquisition of strategic nuclear warheads and delivery vehicles posed, against which no effective defense was considered to be possible. Hence, deterrence by means of punishment became the only option for addressing the new threat. With this was coupled the perception that a conventional defense of Western Europe was either impossible or ruinously expensive (or would result, in any case, in unacceptable levels of destruction to the nations on whose territories the battle would have to be fought).[2] In this context, the predominance of punishment over defense (or denial) as a means of effecting deterrence is not surprising.

Deterrence theory also developed in the context of U.S. containment policy, which sought to prevent any further expansion of Soviet control beyond the line the Red Army had reached in its advance on Germany. Thus, in principle at least, any Soviet military advance was to be deterred.[3] The problem became one of figuring out what kinds

---

[1]Thus, Snyder begins by asserting:

> The central theoretical problem in the field of national security policy is to clarify and distinguish between the two central concepts of *deterrence* and *defense*. . . . Deterrence does not vary directly with our capacity for fighting wars effectively and cheaply; a particular set of forces might produce strong deterrent effects and not provide a very effective denial and damage-alleviating capability. Conversely, forces effective for defense might be less potent deterrents than other forces which were less efficient for holding territory and which might involve extremely high war costs if used. (Snyder, 1961, pp. 3–4; emphasis in the original.)

Later, however, Snyder does recognize the possibility of deterrence by denial:

> It is useful to distinguish between deterrence which results from capacity to deny territorial gains to the enemy, and deterrence by the threat and capacity to inflict nuclear punishment. Denial capabilities—typically, conventional ground, sea, and tactical air forces—deter chiefly by their effect on . . . the aggressor's . . . estimate of the probability of gaining his objective. Punishment capabilities—typically, strategic nuclear power for either massive or limited retaliation—act primarily on . . . the aggressor's estimate of possible costs, and may have little effect on his chances for territorial gain. (Snyder, 1961, pp. 14–15).

[2]The deterrence of a Soviet strategic nuclear attack on the United States, on the one hand, and of a Soviet conventional attack on Western Europe, on the other, became the archetypes of "direct" and "extended" deterrence (using the terminology of Huth, 1988, pp. 16–18.)

[3]Of course, things did not always work out this way in practice, most noticeably in the case of Korea; a statement by then–Secretary of State Dean Acheson in early 1950 describing the U.S. "defense perimeter" in case of general war in the Asia-Pacific

of threats could serve as credible deterrents, once the Soviet Union had broken the American monopoly on nuclear weapons and the ability to deliver them to intercontinental distances. In particular, the threat of nuclear retaliation against the Soviet Union—the heart of the Eisenhower-era doctrine of "massive retaliation"—became less credible once the Soviets could respond in kind, and it seemed to be limited to circumstances involving the highest stakes, e.g., the defense of Western Europe.

It seems clear that any deterrence posture adopted toward China would differ in many important respects. First of all, there is the question of what the United States would be trying to deter. In the Soviet case, deterrence was directed primarily against any future territorial expansion by military means. Although the formative experiences (e.g., the Communist coup d'état in Czechoslovakia, the Berlin blockade, and the North Korean invasion of South Korea) were not actual Soviet military invasions, they did involve the threat or actual use of military forces. The containment policy implied that territorial expansion was the threat to be dealt with and that blocking that expansion would put intolerable pressures on the Soviet regime, leading to its ultimate transformation or destruction.[4]

With respect to China, the overall emphasis would be somewhat different. The initial question is, to what extent does Chinese expansionism have to be deterred in the first place? On the one hand, the Chinese, unlike the Soviets, claim territories (Taiwan, the South China Sea region, and the Senkaku/Diaoyu islands) over which they do not exercise *de facto* control; with respect to these territories, the Chinese claim a right to use force. The U.S. position on the Taiwan issue—that it has "an abiding interest that any resolution be peace-

region could have been interpreted as expressing a disinterest in the fate of the South Korean regime. See Tsou (1963), pp. 535–536.

[4]In his famous article, George Kennan (writing anonymously) advocated "a policy of firm containment, designed to confront the Russians with unalterable counter-force at every point where they show signs of encroaching upon the interests of a peaceful and stable world." This was not, however, a purely defensive policy of "holding the line and hoping for the best." Instead, Kennan argued that, by following such a policy, the United States could

increase enormously the strains under which Soviet policy must operate, . . . force upon the Kremlin a far greater degree of moderation and circumspection . . . , and in this way . . . promote tendencies which must eventually find their outline in either the break-up or the gradual mellowing of Soviet power. ("X" [Kennan], 1947, pp. 581–582.)

ful" (DoD, 1998, p. 35)—implies an interest in deterring any Chinese threat or use of force against Taiwan. Hence, this is one case of possible Chinese territorial expansion that the United States might wish to deter militarily.[5]

With respect to the South China Sea, the United States has not taken any position regarding the overlapping claims of China, Taiwan, and the littoral states to various islands and sectors and has not taken any action to deter or counter unilateral actions by China (or any other claimant) to assert control over any of the disputed islands. Thus, in January 1974, the United States did not come to the aid of its foundering ally when the Chinese seized South Vietnamese–held islands of the Paracel (Xisha) group. Similarly, the United States did not react to the Chinese occupation of Philippine-claimed Mischief Reef in 1995.

However, on June 16, 1995 (after the Chinese had built a permanent structure on Mischief Reef, also claimed by the Philippines), then–Assistant Secretary of Defense for International Security Affairs Joseph Nye said that, if military action in the Spratlys interfered "with freedom of the seas, then we would be prepared to escort and make sure that free navigation continues."[6] Given such a policy, the United States *might*, at some point in the future, seek to deter Chinese military action in the South China Sea on the grounds that it would interfere with navigation along the vital sea routes between the Middle East and East Asia. More recently, in the context of the accession of the Philippines to a Visiting Forces Agreement regularizing the status of U.S. troops temporarily in the country (in the aftermath of the closure of the major U.S. bases at Clark Field and Subic Bay), U.S. Secretary of Defense William Cohen made a statement that was interpreted in the Philippine press as suggesting that the U.S.-Philippines Mutual Defense Treaty could lead to U.S. support for Philippine forces defending claims in the South China Sea.[7]

---

[5]One could debate whether this should be called "territorial expansion"; as used here, the term refers merely to the *de facto* attempt of a government to take control of additional territory beyond what it actually possesses.

[6]Secretary Nye is quoted in Holloway (1995), p. 22.

[7]It is unclear whether Secretary Cohen meant to change U.S. policy in any respect; it is significant that his remarks do not appear to have been reported in the U.S. media. The Philippine press report claimed that "The United States gave its assurance that it

Aside from these cases, it does not appear that the United States will be primarily concerned with deterring Chinese *territorial expansion* in the foreseeable future. The Chinese have territorial claims against several of their neighbors but have not prosecuted the claims, even when a favorable opportunity to do so arose. When China has invaded its neighbors (India in 1962 and Vietnam in 1979), it unconditionally withdrew from the territories it had conquered. Indeed, in 1962, it unilaterally withdrew from conquered territory in northeastern India, despite the fact that it formally claimed the territory in question as rightfully belonging to it. Its border skirmishes with the Soviet Union in 1969 involved islands that it could claim under the "unequal" treaties between the Tsarist and Chinese empires, although its formal stance was that the treaties were invalid and that China could rightfully claim vast areas of the Russian Far East. For the moment, therefore, the possible necessity to deter Chinese military expansion would seem to be limited to Taiwan and the South China Sea, although this, of course, could change as China develops economically and technologically and its "comprehensive national power" increases.

This limited concern with territorial expansion does not, of course, exhaust the range of possible Chinese actions that the United States might wish to deter. More likely, the United States will be concerned with Chinese attempts to use force, military demonstrations, or the threat of force to influence the policies of neighboring states. For example, the missile tests and other military exercises that China conducted in 1995 and 1996 in the Taiwan Strait were designed to rein in Taiwanese President Lee Teng-hui's active diplomacy and to influence the island's legislative and presidential elections. The United States eventually responded by sending two carrier battle groups to the vicinity of Taiwan. In the future, the United States might wish to deter such demonstrations of military force, if possible, either to prevent them from taking place at all or, after they have

will come to the aid of the Philippines in case its forces are attacked in disputed territories in the South China Sea." (Deocadiz, 1998.) While the United States holds that the Mutual Defense Treaty applies only to Philippine territory as it existed in 1951 (and does not cover Philippine-claimed regions of the South China Sea), the Philippine press interpreted Secretary Cohen's remarks to mean that the treaty would apply in case Philippine armed forces came under attack, whether or not they were inside the boundaries of the Philippines, as defined for purposes of the treaty.

begun, to limit their scope (and hence their ability to exert the intended influence).[8]

More generally, in the context of a future conflictual Sino-U.S. relationship, the United States might wish to limit China's influence over its neighbors. It is possible that a future China, as the largest military power in the region, might be willing to use military power to back up its demands that East Asian states pay heed to Chinese interests in determining their foreign policy, including their policy toward the United States. To preserve its political and economic access to East Asia, the United States might seek to deter the Chinese from exerting military pressure of one sort or another. For example, in the context of Korean unification or a thoroughgoing reconciliation between North and South Korea, China might seek the removal of U.S. forces from the Korean peninsula and use military pressure to attain that end, while the United States might seek to deter such Chinese activity.

---

[8]These events are discussed in greater detail in the appendix.

Chapter Five

DETERRENCE AND ITS DISCONTENTS

Recent decades have seen a vast proliferation of writings on deterrence theory, some of it suggesting that deterrence theory was "weaker" (in both descriptive and normative terms) and less useful than had been thought. In addition, even in its more classic formulations, deterrence theory recognized various difficulties in applying it. The future Sino-U.S. context will illustrate many of the perceived weaknesses and criticisms; deterrence theory will be, in general, more difficult to apply than it was in the U.S.-Soviet Cold War context. A review of the deterrence literature suggests four areas of theoretical concerns that would be relevant to deterrence in a Sino-U.S context.[1]

COMMITMENT AND RATIONALITY

Since deterrence primarily relies on the threat of future harm, the deterrer's credibility is obviously a key factor in making deterrence work. If deterrers could inflict the threatened harm at absolutely no cost to themselves, the credibility of their threats could perhaps be taken for granted. It is, however, difficult to think of circumstances in which this would be the case. Hence, the problem of credibility becomes that of convincing the target that the deterrer is willing to bear the costs involved in inflicting the threatened harm. In short,

---

[1]It is obviously impossible to review here all the relevant literature, and, in any case, this report does not aspire to a theoretical treatment of issues in deterrence theory. The points raised in this chapter are those that seem particularly relevant to Sino-U.S. relations. For the same reason, I have not made explicit the links between this discussion and particular critiques of deterrence theory.

deterrers must demonstrate their "commitment" to make good their threats in case deterrence fails (that is, if the one to be deterred takes the undesired action anyway).

Importance of the U.S. Stakes Involved

Credibility may be determined by many factors; one of the most important is the importance to the deterrer of the stakes involved. In the Cold War cases of deterrence, the stakes involved were often large, and their importance was often relatively obvious. Thus, in deterring a Soviet attack on Western Europe, the United States did not face a major problem in conveying the sense that it regarded the stakes as very high: The loss of Western Europe would clearly have been a major blow. Not only did the Western European countries possess major economic, technological, and military capabilities, but the historical, cultural, and ideological ties were also strong. The magnitude of the negative impact of a Soviet conquest of Western Europe on the United States would have been incalculably large. Hence, the threat to use even nuclear weapons in the defense of Western Europe was generally regarded as credible.[2]

In the Sino-U.S. context, however, the importance of the stakes involved in many of the potential deterrence situations may not be so clear. Hence, the United States may find it more difficult to convey the sense that it regards the stakes as high enough to justify the high costs that inflicting threatened punishments might incur.

In the most important case, the United States would wish to deter Chinese use of force against Taiwan. However, this would not necessarily involve any change in its "one China" policy, which implies that the U.S. interest is only in the means by which Taiwan and China might be unified. So, according to this policy, the United States is willing to accept the strategic consequences of Taiwan's incorporation into the PRC (e.g., that Taiwanese ports could become

---

[2]Even in this case, there were many skeptics who doubted, to use the standard cliché, that the United States would risk Chicago to save Paris. Presumably, whatever credibility the threat had rested on the idea that the loss of Western Europe to the Soviet Union would so upset the (physical and ideological) balance of forces between the United States and the USSR that Chicago, and the rest of the United States, would, eventually, be threatened as well.

bases for the Chinese People's Liberation Army Navy). Thus, the United States would have to convince China that, despite its apparent unconcern with the *strategic substance* of reunification, its interest in the *process* is substantial enough to lead the United States to incur large costs. The Chinese leadership might not find such a distinction credible; thus, it might believe either that the United States would not fight or that its willingness to fight indicated a shift in U.S. policy toward actual support for Taiwanese independence. In the latter case, the Chinese might be difficult to deter because of a belief that the result of their forbearance might well be not a continuation of the status quo but rather an invigorated Taiwanese push for independence.[3]

Furthermore, the U.S. insistence that reunification be peaceful and voluntary may not provide an absolutely clear standard in some cases: How much Chinese "saber rattling" would call into question the voluntariness of the Taiwanese decisionmaking process? The United States may find it hard to draw a clear line separating "acceptable" Chinese pressure on Taiwan from what it would seek to deter by means of some sort of retaliation.

The United States would confront a similar problem in trying to deter Chinese use of force in the South China Sea against the other claimants. By not taking a position on the overlapping claims, the United States is in effect saying that Chinese possession of the Paracel and Spratly islands is not incompatible with vital U.S. strategic interests. The U.S. problem, therefore, would be to convince China that our interest in the peacefulness of the determination of ownership of the islands is sufficient to run the risks inherent in the use of force.[4]

---

[3]Of course, this hard-headed realist view (i.e., the view that when a country, such as the United States, claims to be acting on the basis of principle, e.g., that reunification must be peaceful, it is really acting on the basis of its own interests) may simply lead the Chinese to doubt the sincerity of U.S. adherence to a "one China" policy in the first place. The frequent complaint that the United States has a "containment" policy toward China implies that the United States would oppose reunification of China and Taiwan under any circumstances, whether or not it was peaceful.

[4]The difficulty would be compounded by the absence of any U.S. response to past Chinese actions in the South China Sea, even when directed against the Philippines.

On the other hand, if the Chinese actions in the South China Sea appeared to create a serious threat to the freedom of navigation through the area, more-traditional and weighty U.S. interests would be involved. In that case, a U.S. reaction would be more credible. Of course, China would seek to avoid just such a situation by disclaiming any intent to interfere with navigation and perhaps even taking steps, such as the suppression of piracy, to protect it.

The U.S. ability to demonstrate the strength of its interest in deterring Chinese military pressure against regional states might depend not only on the nature of the pressure (how blatant, whether the military activity was confined to Chinese soil, etc.) but also on what it was intended to accomplish. Thus, Chinese pressure on Japan (or South Korea, or a unified Korea) to abandon its alliance with the United States would involve major U.S. interests, thereby making a strong U.S. response more credible. On the other hand, military pressure on Vietnam related to a peripheral issue (such as the disputed border between the two countries) would not seem to engage any important U.S. interest and would thus make a possible U.S. reaction less credible.

The long history of the U.S. alliance with South Korea, as well as its importance for the security of Japan, would presumably make it relatively easy for the United States to make credible its interest in deterring a Chinese invasion of Korea. However, if there were to be a postunification estrangement between Korea and the United States (due perhaps to a nationalist reaction against the continued basing of U.S. troops on the peninsula), China might regard the U.S. stake as considerably reduced. Nevertheless, as long as the U.S.-Japanese alliance remains, it should not be difficult for the United States to convey the strategic importance it attaches to Korea.

Manipulating the Level of "Commitment"

Closely related to the question of defining and measuring the stakes of the parties in a potential conflict is the question of assessing the strength of a side's "commitment" to having its way with respect to the issue. To a large extent, the strength of commitment reflects the importance of the stakes. However, the degree of commitment can be increased, either because of circumstances or as a result of deliberate manipulation, giving the side whose commitment is strengthened a relative bargaining advantage.[5]

To return to the Cold War example as an illustration, the U.S. stakes involved in the defense of Western Europe were inherently enormous. The same, however, could not be said of the defense of West Berlin, an isolated and indefensible outpost whose economy depended on generous West German subsidies. Nevertheless, it acquired symbolic value as an indication of the West's insistence on defending its rights under the four-power agreements reached at the end of World War II and because of the West Berliners' struggle to avoid communist rule; this symbolic value was deliberately magnified by such actions as President Kennedy's visit in the aftermath of the construction of the Berlin Wall.[6] As a result, a half-city that might perhaps have been abandoned without untoward consequences at the start of the Cold War had become an absolutely vital interest by the time of the Cuban missile crisis in 1962.

The PRC leadership's discussion of the Taiwan issue under the rubric of protecting territorial integrity has a similar effect of increasing the value of the stake; the definitive loss of a territory it has never ruled would thereby be transmuted into a humiliating defeat. In general, playing on nationalist sentiment may tie a government's hand in such a case: By emphasizing the importance of Taiwan, the Chinese leadership might make it impossible to ignore any moves toward independence even if it wanted to, for fear that the blow to its prestige would cause it to be toppled from power.[7]

---

[5]The idea is deliberately to raise the cost to oneself of giving in; at the extreme, one would wish to make it impossible for oneself to give in, provided, of course, that this fact could be convincingly conveyed to one's opponent. The ultimate tactic in this regard is Herman Kahn's famous advice for winning the game of "chicken": One convinces one's opponent to swerve first from the center of the road "by getting into the car dead drunk, wearing very dark glasses, and conspicuously throwing the steering wheel out of the window as soon as the car has gotten up to speed." (Kahn, 1962, p. 45.)

[6]Kennedy's speech during that visit is best known for the phrase, "*Ich bin ein Berliner*," which (although usually remembered out of context) engaged his personal prestige in a most indelible manner.

[7]In the past century, popular nationalist pressures have often weakened those in power, when they appeared to be unable to defend China's interests sufficiently vigorously.

On the other hand, PRC leadership has been willing to shelve the Taiwan issue, seemingly indefinitely, for example, in the course of the rapprochement with the United States in 1971–1972.[8] Thus, should it decide that it is was necessary to achieve reunification within a specific time (perhaps because it came to think that time was not on its side and that the overall trend was toward Taiwanese *de jure* independence), it might have some difficulty establishing that it no longer possessed its earlier patience with respect to this issue.

Domestic political considerations could also raise the importance of the Taiwan issue to an American administration. In both cases, the differences between American and Chinese political systems might make it hard to gauge exactly how much domestic pressure the other side's leadership was under.

Defining the "Status Quo"

It is generally believed that the side defending the status quo has a certain advantage.[9] With respect to the issue of credibility, this can be easily understood: It seems plausible to believe that giving up something one possesses will do more damage to one's prestige than failing to attain something to which one aspires. Thus, other things being equal, the "status quo" power may have an edge with respect to credibility.

However, with respect to the potentially most serious source of Sino-U.S. conflict, i.e., Taiwan, the status quo is complex and may be understood differently by the two sides. Taiwan is currently independent *de facto* but enjoys only limited sovereignty *de jure*. It has normal diplomatic relations with only a handful of states, none of

---

[8]Kissinger (1979), p. 1062, quotes Mao as saying: "We can do without them [Taiwan] for the time being; and let it come after 100 years."

[9]See, for example, the discussion of deterrence and compellence in Schelling (1966), pp. 71–73. Jervis (1979), pp. 297–299, discusses in detail the question of whether the defender of the status quo necessarily has an advantage with respect to credibility; he concludes that the defender probably does have an advantage, but that the issue is more complicated than is often thought. In particular, he notes the burden the "aggressor" would have to bear in trying to make credible the claim that a status quo with which he has in fact lived for years is now so intolerable to him that he is willing to run large risks to change it. This, in essence, would be China's problem if it sought to impose a deadline for the unification of Taiwan with the mainland.

them the world's major powers. It has only limited representation in international bodies, and then often under humiliating conditions (such as being unable to call itself by its official name). Most importantly, its main international supporter, the United States, has stated that its arms sales to it will be limited.[10]

Thus, the two sides may emphasize different aspects of the current situation, the United States focusing primarily on Taiwan's *de facto* independence, and China focusing on the nearly universal recognition of the "one China" principle and on Beijing's right to represent that China. If a future Chinese threat to Taiwan arose out of some action by the latter that sought to give a degree of legal or diplomatic expression to its *de facto* independence,[11] each side (China and the United States) could see itself as essentially defending the status quo and could believe that its deterrent threats gained credibility from that circumstance.

"SALAMI TACTICS"

Deterrence typically seeks to clarify the actions by the adversary that are to be deterred, i.e., to specify the actions to which the deterrer will respond by inflicting some form of punishment on the aggressor.[12] In some cases, this clarity may be relatively easy to obtain.

---

[10]"United States–China Joint Communiqué on United States Arms Sales to Taiwan," August 17, 1982, as reprinted in Harding (1992), pp. 383–385. A statement by President Ronald Reagan, issued simultaneously with the communiqué, asserted that

> We attach great significance to the Chinese statement ... regarding China's "fundamental" policy [to strive for a peaceful solution to the Taiwan question], and it is clear from our statements that our future actions will be conducted with this peaceful policy fully in mind. (Harding, 1992, p. 386.)

[11]Such as President Lee Teng-hui's statement in July 1999 that future discussions between China and Taiwan should be on a "special state-to-state" basis.

[12]It is sometimes argued that ambiguity about which actions are to be deterred is a better deterrent than clarity. It is hard to understand how this can be the case; why should a potential aggressor give more weight to an ambiguous threat of retaliation than to a clear one? This is not to argue, however, that ambiguity might not make sense as a *policy* under certain conditions. For example, ambiguity about the set of actions against which one would retaliate might lead an aggressor to desist from an action against which, however undesirable one believes it to be, one would in fact *not* be willing to retaliate. Thus, one gains a deterrent effect without having to make a clear threat that, in the event, one would be reluctant or unwilling to carry out. Similarly, ambiguity may enable one to exert a deterrent effect in circumstances in which

Thus, in the case of a well-demarcated territorial boundary, one could assert that *any* movement of the aggressor's military forces across it would provoke a retaliatory action.

In other cases, however, it may be harder to make clear and credible deterrent threats that cover all possible adversary actions that one wishes to prevent. One study of the successes and failures of U.S. deterrence attempts concluded that

> *Nations interested in changing the status quo normally have more than one option for doing so.* . . . The defender's strategy must be made relevant to the *range* of alternative options possibly available to the initiator. A deterrence policy which discourages an opponent from employing some options but not others is incomplete and may not prevent a failure of deterrence. An opponent who is bent upon altering a given status quo may design around the viable aspects of the deterrence strategy that confronts him. That is, he may seek to formulate an option for challenging the status quo that takes advantage of loopholes, weaknesses, or uncertainties that he perceives in the deterrence strategy of the defending power. (George and Smoke, 1974, pp. 520–521; emphasis in the original.)

Such a strategy has been dubbed *salami tactics*: Rather than making a grab for the entire salami, the aggressor takes a series of thin slices, calibrated so that none of them is sufficiently big to trigger a response by the defender. But, eventually, the aggressor winds up with the entire salami.

Similarly, the aggressor may limit himself to actions whose effects he regards as controllable, i.e., he always leaves himself a way out if his action should trigger a strong response. The study referred to above concluded that

> In almost every historical case [of deterrence failure] examined, we found evidence that the initiator tried to satisfy himself before acting that the risks of the particular option he chose could be calculated and, perhaps even more importantly, *controlled by him* so as to give his choice of action the character of a rationally calculated, acceptable risk. (George and Smoke, 1974, p. 527; emphasis added.)

---

one finds it disadvantageous or impossible, because of public opinion (or the opinion of one's allies), to make a clear threat. This was roughly the situation in which President Eisenhower found himself in 1954–1955 and 1958 with respect to a possible Chinese invasion of the offshore islands of Jinmen (Quemoy) or Mazu (Matsu).

As the historical record recounted in the previous chapter illustrates, China has been adept at calculating and controlling risks in this fashion. Thus, for example, for eight months in 1954–1955, the Chinese shelled the Taiwanese-held offshore islands of Jinmen and Mazu and used military force to take the Yijiangshan Islands (located along the Chinese coast several hundred miles north of Taiwan) from Taiwan, without suffering any military retaliation from the United States, despite the clear disparity in military strength in favor of the latter. Regardless of how one views the political-military outcome of the crisis, the PRC's ability to act provocatively but nevertheless remain beneath the U.S. threshold of military response is striking.

PERCEPTIONS OF THE BALANCE OF FORCES

To deter an adversary, one must possess not only credibility but military capability as well; the will to inflict punishment is obviously irrelevant if the ability to do so is absent. With respect to nuclear deterrence during the latter part of the Cold War, each side's military capability to inflict tremendous damage on the other was relatively well understood. In particular, the existence of nuclear weapons and ballistic missiles, along with the absence of effective ballistic missile defense, made it seem relatively easy to calculate the damage one country could do to the other if it wished to.[13]

Despite arms control–driven reductions, the United States retains enough strategic nuclear strength that its ability to do unacceptable damage to China cannot be questioned. The Chinese nuclear threat to the United States, while much smaller, is likely to grow in the future; even now, it is able to hold a substantial part of the U.S. population at risk. However, for the reasons noted above, either side's willingness to use nuclear weapons, given that it could not entirely escape nuclear retaliation, may well be in doubt in most cases.

From time to time, depending on the issue at stake, one side or the other may try to convey the sense that it would be willing to use nuclear weapons in support of its objectives. For example, prior to the 1996 Chinese missile exercises aimed at intimidating Taiwan, a

---

[13]Earlier in the Cold War, Soviet secrecy and deception efforts combined with U.S. intelligence gaps made it difficult at times for the United States to assess Soviet strategic nuclear power.

Chinese official told a quasi-official American visitor, former Assistant Secretary of Defense Charles Freeman, that China felt it could use force against Taiwan with impunity because American leaders "care more about Los Angeles than they do about Taiwan."[14] Similarly, during a future crisis over Taiwan, the United States might seek to convince China that the issue was important enough to the United States that the use of nuclear weapons could not be ruled out.[15] In general, however, these types of threats are likely to appear disproportionate to the interests at stake: Thus, the relevant question for deterrence may relate to the sides' conventional forces.

Assessments of relative conventional military capabilities, such as would be relevant to judge one side's ability to carry out threatened military actions, are more difficult; the actual use of military forces always carries with it the possibility of unforeseen occurrences. Although overall U.S. military power vastly exceeds that of China, both now and, in all likelihood, during the first decades of the 21st century, the U.S. ability to conduct specific operations at acceptable cost to itself may be difficult to assess. In addition, in the case of a future Sino-U.S. deterrent relationship, the usual difficulties are increased by a number of factors, both military and political.

Militarily, it might be difficult to predict the result of a future Sino-U.S. clash using new weapon systems that have not been used in combat. The Chinese might believe that, despite overall U.S. superiority, a surprise attack by large numbers of short-range ballistic missiles might be able to inflict serious damage on U.S. power-projection capabilities, thereby producing a serious psychological shock that would hamper or even preclude further U.S. action. Even if this were a miscalculation on their part, the result could be that, contrary to U.S. expectations, the Chinese would not be deterred by the presence of a powerful U.S. force in their vicinity, any more than the Japanese were deterred by the forward deployment of the U.S. Pacific Fleet at Pearl Harbor.

This suggests that U.S. force deployments should also be evaluated on the basis of how they would affect Chinese perceptions (as well as

---

[14]The Chinese official's comment appears in Tyler (1996).

[15]This would probably be possible only if Sino-U.S. relations had already deteriorated to something approaching Cold War–style hostility.

in strictly military terms). For example, a more robust deterrent posture might include, in addition to deployments into the immediate theater, forces deployed forward from the United States but at a greater distance from China, to reduce the risk of a massive surprise attack on them.

Politically, the deterrent value of the overall U.S. military superiority might be diminished by a Chinese belief that various political constraints will inhibit the ability of the United States to use it. Given their strategic nuclear capability, the Chinese may believe that the United States would not conduct even conventional attacks against strategic targets in China in retaliation for Chinese actions that do not threaten vital U.S. interests. More generally, the Chinese may believe that U.S. sensitivity to casualties will limit U.S. military actions. Hence, the Chinese perception of usable U.S. military strength may be very different from what the United States might believe.

"STRATEGIC CULTURE"

Deterrence rests, not so much on the deterrer's will and ability to use military force, as on its adversary's perceptions of them. These perceptions are determined not only by the objective realities as a neutral, dispassionate observer might determine them but also by a whole host of cultural factors. If the party to be deterred does not perceive the deterrer's will and ability to act in the intended manner, deterrence may unexpectedly (from the deterrer's point of view) fail.

In general, deterrence theory suggests that military capabilities should be made visible to the adversary, who can then calculate the damage they can do to him and can make his decisions accordingly. In the ideal case, the calculations are made correctly, and then one or the other party, realizing that the military situation is unfavorable, avoids taking steps that would lead to armed conflict.

For example, the United States often believes that the forward deployment of its forces (for example, the movement of aircraft carrier battle groups to waters adjacent to the country to be deterred) sends a strong signal of its ability and willingness to use force in a given situation and thus expects it to have a strong deterrent effect. However, such an action could easily be misinterpreted by a country, such as China, whose strategic tradition emphasizes the importance of surprise attacks. From such a perspective, the deliberate parading of forces might seem more like an alternative to their use; after all, if the adversary had intended to attack, it would have been more discreet about its preparations to do so.

Similarly, the United States might see the absence of visible preparations for the use of force as a sign that its adversary lacks the will or the capability; instead, it might reflect the adversary's desire to achieve surprise when it did in fact attack. Similarly, both the United States (in Korea in 1950) and India (in 1962) misinterpreted a tactical Chinese "pause" (i.e., cessation of armed combat following an initial Chinese attack) as a sign that the Chinese were unwilling or unable to fight a major engagement.

Chapter Six

DETERRING CHINA IN THE FUTURE

THE DIFFICULTY OF DETERRING CHINESE USE OF FORCE

The historical record indicates that China's adversaries often misunderstand its motives and willingness to use force, which affects their ability to deter the Chinese use of force. In Korea, for example, U.S. misunderstanding of China's motives undermined its ability to deter Chinese intervention. U.S. assurances, e.g., that it would not harm the Yalu River hydroelectric plants, showed that it had failed to understand the extent to which the Chinese view of its international situation was tinged by a fearfulness that had a strong ideological component. Thus, Mao's acceptance of the notion of an inevitable (ideologically based) U.S. antagonism to a communist China changed his calculus of the gains and risks of intervening in Korea in a way not understood in Washington. As Christensen has noted,

> it has become common in political science to label leaders in crises as either aggressive and insatiable or fearful and protective of the status quo. The distinction is often useful, but there is no reason to believe that leaders cannot be both aggressive and fearful. Mao was no lover of the status quo, as was proven by his material support to Kim Il-sung and the Vietnamese Communists even before the outbreak of the Korean War; but Mao was also almost paranoid in his feeling of insecurity about threats to his nation, as was demonstrated by his constant fear of foreign and domestic enemies. This type of leader is extremely difficult to deter. If one shows too little resolve, as the United States did by excluding South Korea from the defense perimeter in early 1950, the leader will promote aggression. ... But if one shows too hostile a posture, as the United States did by intervening in the Taiwan Straits, the leader will become panicky,

difficult to reassure, and capable of rash action. (Christensen, 1996, p. 254.)

Success Has Required Very High-Level Threats

For this reason, successful deterrence of China has often required the threat of very high levels of violence. In the 1954–1955 Taiwan Strait crisis, for example, the United States resorted to threats of nuclear attack to deter further Chinese use of force with respect to the offshore islands and to bring about a final cessation of hostile action (e.g., shelling).[1] Similarly, to deter the Chinese instigation of border conflicts in 1969, the Soviets resorted to implicit nuclear threats and to a threat to "destabilize" Xinjiang by supporting Uighur nationalism.

It is unclear whether the United States will be willing or able to make these types of threats in the future. In the absence of a "Cold War" climate of ideological conflict, the United States may not regard the stakes as sufficiently high to threaten nuclear attack, especially given that China now possesses a capability to retaliate with nuclear weapons. It is harder to assess the likelihood and credibility of a possible U.S. threat to play on Chinese internal divisions. Unlike the Soviets' capabilities in 1969, the United States lacks important assets: a common border with regions in which separatist sentiment exists, historical ties to the groups involved, and a reputation for being able to manage these types of operations effectively. On the other hand, the United States can bring to bear much greater public pressure, e.g., by raising the international profile of the Tibetan issue. However, this capability may not be a useful deterrent: Since it depends upon a public campaign, U.S. officials may not be able to assure China that the pressure would be called off if China refrained from

---

[1]Whether or not the United States deterred a Chinese *invasion* of the offshore islands depends, of course, on whether the Chinese had any intention of seizing them. A strong case can be made that the PRC had no interest in taking the offshore islands separately from Taiwan, since that could have facilitated the growth of independence sentiment on Taiwan and the adoption of a "two Chinas" policy on the part of the United States. On the other hand, if the loss of the offshore islands were to lead to a collapse of Nationalist morale on Taiwan (as the Eisenhower administration feared), it could have been very much in the PRC's interest to invade them. Stolper (1985), pp. 9–10, emphasizes the first possibility, but the Eisenhower administration could not afford to neglect the second.

taking the action the United States was trying to deter. As such, public pressure may be too blunt an instrument to have very much deterrent effect.

Relevance of the Historical Record. The PRC's historical record reflects behavior during a period when the disparity in military force between China and its potential adversaries (the United States and the Soviet Union) was considerably greater than it is now, and when the PRC leadership's worldview—more influenced than it is now by ideological factors—saw the outside world as much more threatening. Hence, one could question how relevant this historical record is to current and future Chinese behavior. It could be argued that since China has become militarily stronger and since its current worldview is unaffected by ideological assumptions, it will become less convinced of the inevitable hostility of the outside world and hence more amenable to the ordinary cost-benefit calculations on which deterrence rests.

While such an evolution is certainly possible, it does not appear to have occurred yet. The notion of inevitable hostility based on ideological grounds has disappeared but seems to have been replaced, at least in part, by the notion of a deep-rooted U.S. hostility, on *Realpolitik* grounds, to any increase in Chinese political-military power.[2] Depending on the strength of this belief, future deterrence efforts directed against China could be subject to some of the same difficulties as in the past.

This might be especially true in the case of a Taiwan scenario, in which any U.S. attempt to deter a significant Chinese use of force against Taiwan (such as a blockade or invasion) could be seen as *ipso facto* evidence of U.S. hostility and a desire to detach Taiwan from China permanently. After all, if the Chinese leadership has decided that the situation requires a major use of force, it likely had concluded that Taiwan was on the brink of moving significantly in the direction of a declaration of independence or of taking some other

---

[2]Wang Jisi, a senior Chinese Americanist, believes that "a vast majority of the Chinese political élite" shares, and will continue to share for many years, a set of fundamental assumptions concerning the U.S. role in world affairs, including that "the United States wants to maximize its national power and dominate the world," and that Americans "believe in 'the law of the jungle,' seeing no other nations as equal partners and attempting to prevent them from rising up." (Wang, 1997, p. 3.)

practically irreversible step (such as acquiring a nuclear capability) designed to make reunification impossible or highly improbable. In such a situation, the U.S. insistence that reunification be accomplished peacefully might seem like a smokescreen for an abandonment of the "one China" policy.

Deterrence by Denial. One exception to this general difficulty of deterrence has been what one might call "deterrence by denial," such as the United States practiced in June 1950 when the Seventh Fleet "neutralized" the Taiwan Strait and thus prevented a Communist attempt to occupy Taiwan and bring the civil war to a definitive end. Once the United States was engaged, it was simply beyond the Chinese capability to achieve their goal, and they did not attempt it. In this sense, this may be called an example of deterrence, albeit a trivial one.

The Problem of Deterring Lower Levels of Violence

If the above analysis is accurate, the main problem to be addressed is that of deterring the Chinese from using force when threats of massive retaliation may not be credible. Given that the Chinese now have a capability, however rudimentary, to strike the United States with nuclear weapons, U.S. nuclear threats against China will be credible only if vital U.S. interests are seen to be involved. At present, it is unclear whether the more likely causes of Sino-U.S. conflict qualify in this regard. One could imagine, for example, a future Chinese threat to Japan that the United States would regard in the same light as the Cold War–era Soviet threat to Western Europe. In general, however, this would seem to imply a deterioration of Sino-U.S. relations to the levels of hostility characteristic of the Cold War, in which the doctrines of nuclear deterrence were developed.

Short of that, the problem will remain that of deterring Chinese threats to use force when the threat to U.S. interests is somewhat less cosmic. In the past, this has proved difficult because the Chinese use of force in such cases has had some particular characteristics that frustrate a simple application of typical deterrence theory.

Chinese Often See Value in Crisis, Tension. The Chinese have often shown a willingness to resort to force precisely because they see the resulting tension as in their interest. It is often claimed that, since *weiji*, the Chinese word for *crisis*, is composed of two characters that can be translated as *danger* and *opportunity*, respectively, it does not have an entirely negative connotation. This is apparently apocryphal[3]; nevertheless, it does appear that, for the Chinese leadership, a crisis is not necessarily a negative phenomenon: It may provide an opportunity for making gains that would otherwise not be achievable.[4] Thus, the creation of a crisis may be a way to probe an adversary's intentions, to cause difficulties between it and its allies, or to weaken its resolve and the domestic political support for its policies.

The purpose of the tension may be domestic mobilization (which is one interpretation of the 1958 Taiwan Strait crisis); alternatively, it may be intended to exert a psychological impact on a foreign power and hence bring about a change in its policies. If the foreign country that is the "target" of the crisis appears undecided or irresolute about an issue, a "demonstration" (involving the actual, but carefully limited, use of force) of the kinds of trouble to which a policy unfavorable to China might lead could be a useful way to affect that country's decisionmaking process.

This type of behavior may be difficult to deter. Threats to use (limited amounts of) force in reply may indeed play into the Chinese strategy. If the object is to create tension, the adversary's counter-threats help rather than hurt, as long as the harm they threaten to cause remains within acceptable bounds. The key notion here seems to be the question of controlling the level of tension and the risk of escalation rather than avoiding them altogether. Hence, a strategy of carefully controlled escalatory threats and actions may be an inappropriate means of achieving a deterrent effect.

Thus, in the Taiwan Strait crisis, the Chinese clearly wanted to create a certain level of tension and the sense, in the United States and elsewhere in the West, that the outbreak of war was possible. It was this tension that put pressure on the U.S. government to resolve the problem: Domestic opinion was perturbed by the possibility of going to war over a handful of small, remote, and seemingly inconsequential islands, while America's European allies feared that the

---

[3]Or so the author understands from a native speaker.

[4]The view that crises are invariably bad—i.e., that they offer "danger" but not "opportunity"—is the understandable perspective of a status quo power, such as the United States, which regards tension as something that must be resolved as soon as possible lest it lead to war, especially nuclear war.

United States would become bogged down on the other side of the globe and hence be a less-effective protector against the Soviet Union. At the same time, as instigators of the crisis, the Chinese felt (in this instance, correctly) that they could control its intensity and avoid its escalation to levels that could be dangerous to them.

SCENARIO: DETERRENCE OF CHINESE USE OF FORCE AGAINST TAIWAN

Of the possible future deterrence scenarios, one of the more likely cases, and potentially the most important one, would be a U.S. attempt to deter China from using force against Taiwan. China has consistently refused to undertake not to use force to achieve reunification with Taiwan; indeed, as Jiang Zemin asserted in a major speech on the topic,

> Such commitment [not to use force] would only make it impossible to achieve peaceful reunification and could not but lead to the eventual settlement of the question by the use of force. (Jiang, 1995.)

The Chinese leadership seems to believe that Taiwan's reluctance to unify with the mainland is such that at least the threat of force will ultimately be necessary to convince it to agree to "peaceful" reunification, even under the "one country, two systems" formula.

Chinese Objectives

Potential Chinese objectives in using force against Taiwan would of course depend on the situation at the time; one could imagine a variety of political circumstances in which the question of Chinese use of force would arise. In some circumstances, initiative would lie with the Chinese as to whether they chose to advance their interests by means of the threat or actual use of force; in others, the Chinese might feel compelled to respond to a Taiwanese action.

With respect to political objectives, the Chinese could seek to

- deter or reverse a Taiwanese "declaration of independence"
- deter Taiwan from developing nuclear weapons or compel it to abandon an ongoing program

- deter or compel the abandonment of U.S.-Taiwanese military cooperation (e.g., an access agreement)

- deter Taiwan from pursuing an "independence-minded" course or influence its electorate not to support candidates favoring such a course

- compel Taiwan to accept reunification.

The cases are listed in terms of the urgency with which China is likely to feel compelled to act. In the case of an actual or imminent formal Taiwanese "declaration of independence," especially if it appeared that other countries might be willing to recognize Taiwan as a new state, China might feel that it had to act immediately or see its claim to sovereignty over the island irretrievably damaged. The prospect of a Taiwanese nuclear capability might prompt a similar reaction, since it could appear to the Chinese to be an effective counter to the credibility of their "background" threat to use force. The timing of a Chinese move could, however, depend on factors other than the precise status of the Taiwanese nuclear program.

The timing of a threat or use of force to deter the Taiwanese government from following an "independence-minded" course of action— the apparent motivation of the missile tests and military exercises in 1995 and 1996—affords China much more flexibility, since such a course of action would take a long time to reach fulfillment. At each step along the way (e.g., the Taiwanese president's unofficial visit to the United States), China would have to decide whether a major reaction was called for or not. Under some circumstances, however, China may feel compelled to act before an election, to head off the victory of a candidate it regarded as committed to independence or to support a candidate it regarded as more favorable to reunification.

Finally, even if the Chinese leadership were to set an internal "deadline" for reunification, as long as that fact were not made public, it would be free to apply pressure to compel reunification on its own timetable. On the other hand, if the deadline were made public, China might feel pressed to take action at an inopportune time, for considerations of prestige, although a face-saving reason for postponing action would not be hard to invent.

Whatever the political motivation, there could be a wide variety of more immediate objectives of the military action. In order of increasing seriousness, the purpose of Chinese military operations could be

- saber rattling for political effect

- harassment designed to cause minor cost or inconvenience, for political effect (e.g., interfering with shipping or air routes, causing detours or delays)

- serious interference with shipping or air routes designed to cause serious economic loss and/or financial panic

- blockade and/or missile bombardment designed to cause surrender

- occupation of the island.

U.S. Commitment: "Strategic Ambiguity"

As already noted, the U.S. commitment to deter any Chinese use of force against Taiwan may not be entirely clear to the Chinese. Indeed, the current U.S. policy is one of "strategic ambiguity," i.e., a deliberate refusal to state explicitly that the United States would defend Taiwan against Chinese attack. This policy derives from the complexity of the fundamental U.S. stance toward Taiwan: support for its *de facto* independence (in the sense of rejection of Chinese use of force to change Taiwan's political status) combined, however, with the rejection, as part of the "Three Noes" policy,[5] of *de jure* independence and "acknowledg[ment of] the Chinese position that there is but one China and Taiwan is part of China."[6] This implies U.S. opposition to any Taiwanese declaration of *de jure* independence and hence the reluctance to provide any security guarantees that might make Taiwan believe that declaring independence was less risky than it would be in the absence of such a guarantee.

Given this complexity, it is difficult to assess how credible the U.S. commitment to defend Taiwan would appear in a given situation. If

---

[5]As stated by President Clinton, June 30, 1998, in Shanghai and reported in Pomfret (1998).

[6]"United States–China Joint Communiqué on United States Arms Sales to Taiwan," August 17, 1982 (reprinted in Harding, 1992, p. 383).

China were reacting to Taiwanese moves that it regarded as "provocative" (because, for example, they appeared to the Chinese as tantamount to a declaration of independence), it might feel that the United States would be politically constrained from reacting militarily.

More generally, China would have to assess the U.S. interest in Taiwan's continued *de facto* independence. This would not be an easy assessment to make. First of all, the formal U.S. position implies that the United States has no *strategic* interest in Taiwan's being independent of the mainland; otherwise, it ought to oppose peaceful reunification as well as reunification by force. Hence, China would have to assess how committed the United States was to the mere *principle* of nonuse of force, as opposed to concern for the object for which force might be used.[7] Second, it might be unclear to China whether the United States would see Chinese use of force against Taiwan as a harbinger of a more aggressive policy generally or whether the United States could be brought around to accept China's view that, Taiwan being an internal affair, China's use of force against it did not signify a policy of future (international) expansionism. Finally, China would have to assess how the United States valued Taiwan relative to its larger concerns vis-à-vis China itself, including its economic interests. To the extent that China was able to control the timing of its use of force against Taiwan, it could attempt to manipulate some of these factors affecting U.S. perceptions, for example, by improving its relations with other East Asian nations, by taking steps to resolve outstanding disputes with them, and/or by raising the value to the United States of Sino-U.S. economic ties (lowering tariffs or other trade barriers, enhancing the security of U.S. economic interests in China, signing major contracts with U.S. corporations, etc.).

U.S. Capability

As discussed above, the United States might seek to deter Chinese military action by appearing able and willing to deny the Chinese the achievement of their military objective or by threatening retaliation.

---

[7]While the Chinese claim to be very principled with respect to their international behavior, they hardly attribute the same virtue to the United States.

Denial. A clear U.S. capability to deny the Chinese the objective for which they might be willing to use force against Taiwan would probably be the most reliable method of deterrence. China would probably believe that the United States would be more willing to use such a capability than one that required the United States to expand the scope of hostilities to include retaliation against Chinese targets not directly related to the use of force against Taiwan.

Assessing whether such a capability exists or will exist in the future is very complicated. Generally speaking, with respect to the lesser military objectives listed above (e.g., saber rattling or harassment), it would appear impossible for the United States to deny the Chinese the ability to achieve their goal.[8] Indeed, the U.S. response itself, if it were perceived as an overreaction by a significant part of the Taiwanese population or by other countries in the region, could contribute to the accomplishment of the Chinese objective by raising tensions higher than they would otherwise have been.

At the higher level (occupation or blockade), China at present may be incapable of achieving its objective even in the absence of U.S. involvement. A clear indication of U.S. willingness to use force would suffice to demonstrate to China that it could not achieve its objective. This favorable situation, however, is likely to erode over the next several decades. Enhanced Chinese capabilities involving short-range missiles (potentially with chemical warheads); surveillance capabilities (especially ocean surveillance); and new, quiet diesel submarines could increase the Chinese ability to achieve these objectives, absent U.S. willingness and ability to commit major forces.[9]

At present, the United States could probably prevent Chinese achievement of the middle objective (inflicting serious economic loss by interfering with shipping and air routes), although there could be

---

[8]According to press reports, former Assistant Secretary of Defense Charles Freeman was told during a trip to China in late 1994 that "the People's Liberation Army had prepared plans for a missile attack against Taiwan consisting of one conventional missile strike a day for 30 days." (Tyler, 1996.) U.S. development of an effective, rapidly deployable, area ballistic missile defense system could provide the capability to deny China the ability to inflict this type of harassment on Taiwan.

[9]See Khalilzad (1999), Ch. 3, for a discussion of the impact of Chinese military modernization.

an initial period of panic on Taiwan before it became evident that the losses the Chinese interference caused would remain in the tolerable range. In the future, this may become more difficult for the reason given above.

Retaliation. The U.S. capability to retaliate with nuclear weapons would seem assured for the foreseeable future. However, this raises all of the "extended deterrence" issues with which the United States struggled during the Cold War. In particular, could a U.S. threat to run the risk of Chinese nuclear retaliation in defense of Taiwan be made credible, given the vast difference between the weight of Taiwan, on the one hand, and Western Europe, on the other, with respect to the global balance of power?

In addition, the United States will likely retain the ability to inflict serious damage on Chinese military and economic targets using conventional air and cruise missile attacks, although the United States would probably not be able to "collapse" the Chinese air defense system the way that it rendered Iraqi air defenses ineffective in Desert Storm. Thus, the ongoing costs of a U.S. retaliation campaign are likely to be relatively high. The size of such a campaign would be affected by the amount of available basing in the region (especially whether basing on Taiwan was feasible).

In addition, political constraints would limit the range of Chinese targets to be attacked: There could be a strong desire to avoid collateral damage, and targets might be limited to military facilities directly involved in the Chinese action against Taiwan. Thus, military targets that the Chinese leadership might care about most, such as nuclear facilities in northwest China, might not be targetable.

Finally, methods of retaliation other than air and missile strikes would be possible. For example, a Chinese attempt to blockade Taiwan could be answered by a U.S. blockade of Chinese ports. This could have wider international repercussions than air strikes on military targets (or a trade embargo by the United States and any other states that chose to join the United States), since it would interfere with other countries' trade with China, but it might otherwise be preferable as a less escalatory (more "tit-for-tat") option.

Retaliation could also take nonmilitary forms, for example, trade sanctions, imposition of strict export controls, or downgrading of diplomatic relations. How successful this would be would depend primarily on whether the other advanced industrial nations were willing to impose similar restrictions on their relations with China. Strict trade sanctions against China on the part of all NATO nations plus Japan and Korea could, in theory, impose a very high cost on the Chinese, since they value economic and technological development highly. However, it seems unlikely that such a threat would have much deterrent value, given the demonstrated inability of these countries to maintain a common front and given the allure of the Chinese market.

Possible Chinese Course of Action

Judged entirely by the historical record, China's use of force against Taiwan would very likely occur at the lower end of the scale in terms of military objectives. In the 1950s, for example, China harassed Taiwanese garrisons on Jinmen and Mazu islands with artillery barrages; in 1995 and 1996, its missile tests and military exercises fell into the same category. Only once (in 1955) did China occupy Taiwanese-held territory; this involved the small, remote (from Taiwan) islands of the Yijiangshan group. Even the late-1994 threat to attack Taiwan directly (passed unofficially to a visiting American former official; see Tyler, 1996) involved the use of only 30 missiles, to be launched at the rate of one a day.

However, future actions may be different, for several reasons. First, the political circumstances may change in a manner unfavorable to China. Assuming the democratization of Taiwan's political life continues, the self-confidence of the society may increase. This may decrease the value of harassment tactics: After several decades of democratic rule, with indigenous Taiwanese (as opposed to mainlanders) holding the major political offices, Taiwanese society may be harder to intimidate. In addition, low-level harassment tactics could backfire in that they might provoke Taiwan to declare independence formally, a danger that would not have existed in the past, when Taiwan's political leadership was adamantly against independence.[10] Hence, to have the same effect, China may have to ratchet up the military pressure it applies.

---

[10]In this connection, it is of interest that, when the Chinese called off the artillery bombardment of the offshore islands in October 1958, one motivation might have

Second, the initiative in the past incidents lay with China, which was able to control the level of tension as it saw fit. In the future, China may find itself faced with a Taiwanese action that appears so provocative that it feels it has no choice but to bring overwhelming pressure to bear to stop it. In particular, the pre-1949 pattern suggests that a weak or unstable regime in Beijing might find itself pushed by popular pressure into taking stronger action than it would have wished.   Indeed, even the current regime has acted—for instance, in response to the actions of private Japanese citizens to affirm sovereignty over the Senkaku/Diaoyutai islands in 1996–1997—as if it feared allowing the free expression of its people's nationalist passions.[11] If the regime felt weaker domestically than it does now, it might, at some future point, feel more compelled to act to satisfy nationalist passions.

Third, a future Chinese leadership may find it harder to call off an unsuccessful attempt to intimidate Taiwan than did past leaderships. In 1958, for example, Mao was able to reverse course dramatically after his attempt to starve out the Nationalist garrisons on Jinmen and Mazu failed; he could rationalize calling off the (unsuccessful) blockade of the islands by suggesting that their abandonment by the KMT would be a step toward the realization of a "two China" policy on the part of the United States.[12] Evidently, he did not feel that the abrupt about-face would cause him to lose prestige domestically; a future Chinese government might not feel so secure and, hence, once embarked on a policy of military pressure against Taiwan, might feel that it had no choice but to escalate the pressures until it succeeded in achieving its originally stated goal.

---

been the fear that the crisis risked abetting a "two China" policy putatively being pursued by the United States. As Anna Louise Strong, presumably speaking for high Chinese officials, wrote: "To take [Jinmen] at present ... would isolate Taiwan and thus assist [U.S. Secretary of State John Foster] Dulles in his policy of building 'two Chinas.'" (Strong, 1958.)

[11]For example, the *Hong Kong Standard* reported that "Jiang Zemin has ordered university officials to prevent students from staging protests over the Diaoyu islands row." ("Jiang Issues Campus Gag Order on Diaoyu Islands," 1996.) Similar reports appeared in the same newspaper on September 13, 16, and 18.

[12]Whether or not Mao initially intended to take the islands is irrelevant to this point: Even if he had never intended to take them, he had to reckon with the possible public perception of defeat when he did not.

Finally, the military balance may be more favorable to China than it has been in the past; in particular, U.S. military predominance over China will be less complete, given Chinese strategic nuclear weapons and incipient ocean surveillance and strike capabilities. Hence, China may feel that it can use greater levels of military force in putting pressure on Taiwan. Ultimately, if China were ever to believe that it could occupy Taiwan with speed and certainty, thereby presenting the United States with a *fait accompli*, the temptation to solve the reunification issue once and for all might be very great.

U.S. Deterrence Strategy

"Strategic Ambiguity." The current U.S. policy of "strategic ambiguity" is designed to deter Chinese use of force against Taiwan without committing the United States to react in any given case and without running the risk of encouraging the Taiwanese to take actions that the Chinese would see as provocative. It is meant to deter the Taiwanese as well as the Chinese, by leaving both in some doubt as to how the United States would react to any given situation.

While a posture of ambiguity thus reduces certain costs of pursuing a deterrence policy and enables one to achieve a degree of deterrence "on the cheap," it also has potential drawbacks. Essentially, it pays for its advantages by creating a greater risk of miscalculation; the side to be deterred may take certain actions in the mistaken belief that the would-be deterrer will not react, thus perhaps resulting in an "accidental" war that would not have come about had the active side understood clearly the consequences of its actions.

Whatever the theoretical advantages and disadvantages of ambiguity, it would seem to be an inappropriate policy in the long run for deterring Chinese use of force against Taiwan. First, Chinese action against Taiwan may be triggered by events that the Chinese leadership sees as threatening to its core national goals, to say nothing of survival of the regime itself, i.e., events that seem to the Chinese leadership to point clearly toward a Taiwanese assertion of independence. In such a case, the impulse toward taking action will be strong. While ambiguity may be useful in preventing a side from taking actions that it sees as advantageous but not required (why risk serious trouble for something that is not necessary but would be merely nice to have?), it is less likely to prevent actions that a side sees as necessary to protect core values or ensure survival (in which case the choice becomes one of possible trouble if one acts, as opposed to the certainty of serious problems if one does not).

Second, an ambiguous U.S. posture is likely to be interpreted in the light of overall U.S. policy. Thus, a U.S. policy of improving bilateral relations could easily lead China to believe that its freedom of action with respect to Taiwan had been tacitly expanded. In particular, if China were to believe that the United States, in the interest of good relations, had implicitly adopted a favorable stance toward "peaceful" reunification (e.g., by pressing Taiwan to accept "one country, two systems"), it might read a policy of strategic ambiguity as giving it freedom to use at least low levels of force to move reunification forward, to say nothing of opposing Taiwanese steps toward *de jure* independence.[13]

More generally, the more the United States appears to favor good relations with China, the more likely it is that China will interpret a policy of strategic ambiguity in a manner favorable to its freedom of action. Precisely because the United States may seem to have good reasons to want to avoid a conflict with China over Taiwan, the commitment to oppose the use of force against Taiwan must be made explicit. Indeed, the United States would be forced, in this circumstance, to follow the opposite policy, one of seeking ways of making its commitment less flexible and more difficult to "interpret away," to make it clear to China that, even if the United States wanted to abandon Taiwan, the costs in terms of U.S. prestige and credibility would be too high to bear.[14]

As an alternative, the United States could adopt a more clear-cut policy with respect to Taiwan; such a policy would commit the United States to the defense of Taiwan against any Chinese use of

---

[13]This dynamic may have contributed to the Chinese decision to conduct the military exercises of 1996; the Chinese may have been truly surprised by the level of the U.S. military reaction. Garver (1997), pp. 112–113, presents evidence that the Chinese leadership was in fact surprised by the U.S. reaction in 1996.

[14]The standard deterrence literature discusses at length various methods of enhancing deterrence by binding oneself irretrievably to a commitment, thereby making it very difficult or even impossible to wriggle out of it. The classic illustration of this is Herman Kahn's instructions (noted above) for winning a game of "chicken": Ostentatiously throw the steering wheel out the car window before the game begins.

force *unless* Taiwan was judged to have provoked the attack by declaring *de jure* independence, developing nuclear weapons, or taking one or more "provocative" steps, which would have to be spelled out in some detail. While the explicit statement of such a policy might be only that the guarantee would be withdrawn in case Taiwan behaved in a prohibited manner, it would be subject to the interpretation—which might or might not be a misinterpretation— that the United States would *not* defend Taiwan in such a case.

Such a policy would aim to deter Taiwan from taking one of the provocative steps and to deter China from using force against a Taiwan that had not. It would be less subject to Chinese misinterpretation at times when the United States is striving to improve Sino-U.S. relations or when the United States might appear to be less interested in events in East Asia. It would raise the cost to the United States (in terms of prestige and credibility) of not defending Taiwan; to the extent that the Chinese understood and believed this, they would have to take the possibility of a U.S. reaction to their use of force against Taiwan more seriously.

Military Prerequisites. To back up such a policy, the United States should take steps to demonstrate a military capability to counter Chinese uses of force against Taiwan. To the extent possible, a capability to deny the Chinese the ability to attain their military objectives would probably be the most effective deterrent. In particular, such a "blocking" capability would not be subject to a Chinese "counterdeterrent," whereas the Chinese might believe they could inhibit U.S. retaliatory threats by posing threats of the "is Taiwan worth Los Angeles?" variety. Since ballistic missiles represent the main Chinese power-projection capability, as well as its main threat to U.S. assets in the theater, effective theater ballistic missile defense would be the primary means of supporting such an approach.[15]

Even when denial is impossible (as discussed above), the United States would need to demonstrate the military capability of counter-

---

[15]Of course, providing Taiwan with an effective ballistic missile defense, even if possible, would presumably be seen by China as a hostile action. As discussed later, China might see actions aimed at negating China's ability to use force against Taiwan as parts of an implicit or deliberate policy of prolonging Taiwan's separate status indefinitely.

ing the political effect of any Chinese actions. The U.S. willingness to deploy two carrier battle groups near Taiwan during the 1996 crisis played an important role in countering the psychological effect of the Chinese military exercises. Preserving the capability to operate carriers close to Taiwan will be an important military prerequisite of a strong deterrence posture. In addition, demonstrating that the U.S. Air Force will be able to operate over and near Taiwan would be an important means of bolstering deterrence. The various means of doing this (permanent bases, creating the political preconditions for access during a crisis, longer-range fighter aircraft, etc.) have been investigated in other RAND publications. (See Khalilzad, 1999, pp. 77–83, and Stillion and Orletsky, 1999, Chs. 4 and 5.)

Finally, a retaliatory capability remains important. The key point here would be strengthening its credibility in the face of a Chinese counterdeterrence strategy. This is not, strictly speaking, a military issue, although there may be military components.[16] U.S. declaratory policy concerning, for example, which Chinese targets would be considered tactical if force were used against Taiwan (e.g., the ports, air bases, and missile bases from which the attack against Taiwan was launched) could begin the process of creating perceptual "thresholds" between limited homeland attacks and all-out exchanges. Similarly, U.S. policy could suggest an equation between aircraft carriers and air bases.

Fundamental U.S. Policy Issues. As this short discussion makes clear, questions of deterrence must be addressed in the context of fundamental U.S. policy issues regarding Taiwan. Most fundamentally, the United States would have to decide on the relative importance of strengthening deterrence and of pursuing better relations with China. This would directly affect the possibility of abandoning strategic ambiguity in favor of a clearer statement of intent: A clearer policy would make China face the fact that the United States intended to deter Chinese use of force against Taiwan. A corollary of Jiang's statement (at the beginning of this section) would be that successful U.S. deterrence of Chinese use of force against Taiwan

---

[16]For example, the stationing of Pershing IIs and ground-launched cruise missiles in Western Europe in the early 1980s served the primarily political purpose of enhancing the "coupling" between Western Europe and the United States in the face of Soviet strategic nuclear power.

implies the impossibility of "peaceful" reunification. Hence, the United States would either have to allow the Chinese perception that the United States favored indefinite separation to stand or have to take positive steps to promote peaceful reunification.

At the same time, a clearer policy would presumably state some circumstances (at least, an outright declaration of independence) under which the United States would not commit itself to the defense of Taiwan. The Chinese might well interpret this to mean that the United States would *not* defend Taiwan in such a situation. While it may be in the interest of the United States to try to deter Taiwan from taking such provocative actions, it is not clear whether, once Taiwan had done so, the United States would want to abandon it to its fate. Until such a decision had been taken, it might prove impossible to craft a clearer policy than the current one.

Similar considerations would affect the narrower decisions regarding the military steps that could be taken to strengthen deterrence. Any step taken to strengthen deterrence (especially those that involved basing forces on Taiwan or transferring weapons to it) could also be read in Beijing as a step toward an eventual policy of support for indefinite *de facto* or eventual *de jure* independence for Taiwan.

ROLE OF DETERRENCE IN A FUTURE SINO-U.S. RELATIONSHIP

Deterrence theory assumes a certain transparency of intent and capability. In principle, the party to be deterred should be able to calculate the deterrer's willingness to use force and capability to do so with some degree of accuracy, to determine whether or not the deteree should proceed with its desired course of action. In fact, in many historical cases, the reality was quite different; the motives of the parties were opaque, and the strength of their military capabilities was misestimated, often wildly so.

NONMILITARY TYPES OF DETERRENCE

Unless Sino-U.S. relations deteriorate to Cold War–like levels, it would seem that nuclear deterrence will have little role to play in handling the types of conflict scenarios that might arise. If this is so, the record suggests that deterrence at a lower level may be difficult to manage. Indeed, depending on the circumstances, China may see low-level tension as being in its interest.[17]

This poses a difficult but not insurmountable challenge to U.S. policymakers. The key may be to seek nonmilitary means of deterrence, i.e., diplomatic ways to manipulate the tension to China's disadvantage. For example, one interpretation of the Chinese decision to wind down the 1958 Taiwan Strait crisis was that Mao feared that the United States was using the crisis to persuade Chiang Kai-shek to withdraw his troops from the offshore islands, once that could be done in a way that did not look like giving in to Chinese pressure. By thus breaking this link between Taiwan and the mainland, the United States would be promoting a "two China" policy (which Mao feared was the true U.S. goal). So, the crisis could have led to a result very disadvantageous to China; although Mao would have probably been happy to take the offshore islands in a context that humiliated the KMT and the United States, receiving them as a "gift" would be an entirely different matter:

> Available data from August [1958] do not demonstrate that Mao was concerned about the negative repercussions of recovering the islands at the very beginning of the crisis, but Chinese actions and statements show that such concerns were paramount in September and October. A KMT retreat from Quemoy and Matsu would move the Civil War enemy much further (100 miles) from the mainland, making it harder to attack in the future. . . . the delinkage of Taiwan from the mainland would only further the cause of Taiwanese separatism. (Christensen, 1996, p. 231.)

In future crises, China will have to be concerned that its threat or use of force will encourage neighboring states to see her as an emerging

---

[17]A major question, which cannot be addressed here, would concern how China would see such tension affecting its economic development. If China believes that its economic development no longer requires close trade and financial relations with the United States or believes that such ties could survive heightened political-military tension, the way would be open to the use of "demonstrative" force, as in the past. On the other hand, if China believes that political-military tension would create serious economic disadvantages, this would be an important restraint. However, China's economic integration into the world also creates strong economic interests in the United States, which would be hurt by Sino-U.S. tension; hence, China might believe that the prospect of such tension would bring strong domestic pressure to bear on the U.S. government to take whatever steps might be necessary to avoid tension.

strategic threat against which they must band together. Following Chinese actions at Mischief Reef in 1995, for example, the states making up the Association of Southeast Asia Nations drew somewhat closer together in support of the Philippines, one of the members. (Valencia, 1995, pp. 42–43, 45, 48–49.) This type of regional reaction, encouraged and supported by the United States, may be the best deterrent to Chinese use of force in the region.

CHINESE "DETERRENCE" ATTEMPTS: FAILURES AND SUCCESSES

The PRC has at best a mixed record with respect to deterrence attempts in its nearly 50-year history. Although it is hard at times to determine what should count as a deterrence attempt (and, on occasion, it is difficult to know what should count as success), the Chinese have not in general been very successful in deterring actions they regarded as inimical to their interests.

However, it should be noted from the outset that, in most cases, China was trying to deter either a stronger country (the United States or the Soviet Union) or a country closely allied to such a power. The only clear exception to this was the unsuccessful Chinese attempt to deter incursions into disputed border areas by the militarily weaker Indians in the fall of 1962. Even in this instance, however, China was at the time suffering from the consequences of the economically disastrous "Great Leap Forward."

The more important question is, however, whether the PRC leadership understood itself as engaging in deterrence in the sense in which U.S. analysts and practitioners understand the term. As will appear from many of these examples, Chinese military postures and actions have often been structured to favor achieving surprise (and the psychological shock it can produce) rather than enhancing the effectiveness of deterrence.[1] The Chinese concept of deterrence, if one may be spoken of, seems to depend more on the cumulative effect of past actions than on specific threats about the future: By using military force to "teach a lesson" to an adversary, one makes it

---

[1]See Burles and Shulsky (2000) for a discussion of this point.

more likely that he will think twice before acting against one's interests in the future.

Thus, these examples cover cases that, in terms of U.S. strategic thinking, would seem to call for attempts at deterrence; whether one ought to characterize the Chinese behavior in such a way is less clear.

FAILURES[2]

U.S. and UN Troops Cross the 38th Parallel and Advance to the Yalu (Fall 1950)

Thanks to research using recently available internal Chinese documents, we can have a better understanding of the Chinese reaction to the UN victories in Korea in September through November 1950.[3] This helps round out the picture of the multiple failures of deterrence that occurred during that period.

As far as can be determined from the historical record, it appears that, with respect to the crossing of the 38th parallel, the United States was eminently deterrable. Despite earlier statements that implied that the UN goal was the reunification of Korea by force of arms, such as that of the U.S. representative to the UN Security Council on August 17,[4] President Truman approved, in mid-September 1950, a National Security Council recommendation that

> General MacArthur was to conduct the necessary military operations either to force the North Koreans behind the 38th parallel or to destroy their forces. If there was no indication or threat of entry of

---

[2]By referring to these cases as "failures" of Chinese deterrence, I mean only that they are cases in which China's adversary actually did what China wished it would not have. I do not mean to imply that the "blame" for this should be attributed to Chinese policymakers who made "mistakes" that wiser officials would have avoided; in some cases, any "mistakes" that were made might just as easily be laid at the doorstep of the adversary's policymakers. For example, the Chinese intervention in the Korean War is often categorized as an intelligence (rather than a deterrence) failure; such an analysis implies that the real "mistake" was the failure of the United States to be deterred rather than the failure of the Chinese to deter.

[3]Christensen (1992) demonstrates the importance of this new evidence for assessing Mao's Korean War strategy. The discussion in the text draws heavily from this article and from Christensen's 1996 book.

[4]Whiting (1960), p. 78, speaks of the speech's "seeming insistence upon total North Korean defeat as the minimal condition for terminating hostilities."

Soviet or Chinese Communist elements in force, the National Security Council recommended that General MacArthur was to extend his operations north of the parallel and to make plans for the occupation of North Korea. However, no ground operations were to take place north of the 38th parallel in the event of Soviet or Chinese Communist entry. (Truman, 1956, p. 359.)

At the end of the month, according to Truman's memoirs,

> I had already given approval to new instructions which the Joint Chiefs of Staff had transmitted to MacArthur on September 27, in which he was told that his military objective was "the destruction of the North Korean Armed Forces." In attaining this objective he was authorized to conduct military operations north of the 38th parallel in Korea, provided that at the time of such operation there had been no entry into North Korea by major Soviet or Chinese Communist forces, no announcement of intended entry, and no threat by Russian or Chinese Communists to counter our military operations in North Korea. (Truman, 1956, p. 360.)

Thus, as late as the end of September 1950, a credible threat of Chinese intervention could well have prevented U.S. troops from crossing the 38th parallel (although South Korean troops might have moved north on their own). Things changed very quickly, however. On October 1, MacArthur publicly called on North Korea to surrender, and South Korean troops crossed the 38th parallel; U.S. troops followed on October 7.

On the night of October 2–3, Chinese Premier Zhou Enlai called in the Indian ambassador to Beijing, K. M. Panikkar. Panikkar was to tell the United States that if its troops crossed the 38th parallel, China would enter the war. The choice of messenger was unfortunate. According to Truman's memoirs, Panikkar "had in the past played the game of the Chinese Communists fairly regularly, so that his statement could not be taken as that of an impartial observer." (Truman, 1956, p. 362.) In other words, Panikkar's warning was discounted because of his political sympathies; the Chinese message was considered to be a bluff rather than a serious warning.

Of course, more was at work than merely the unfortunate choice of a messenger. MacArthur's brilliant victory with respect to the landing at Inchon on September 15, and the subsequent collapse of the North Korean forces, raised hopes that the Korean problem could be solved once and for all, thereby avoiding the need for a continuing deployment of U.S. troops on the Korean peninsula. China was regarded as militarily too weak to intervene effectively in any case. There was a subtle change in MacArthur's orders:

> Hereafter in the event of open or covert employment anywhere in Korea of major Chinese Communist units, without prior announcement, you should continue the action as long as, in your judgment, action by forces now under your control offers a reasonable chance of success. (Truman, 1956, p. 362.[5])

Mere Chinese intervention (to say nothing of the threat of it) would no longer be sufficient to prevent U.S. troops from operating north of the 38th parallel. Instead, it was left to MacArthur's judgment whether the Chinese forces posed a threat to the accomplishment of his mission. Unstated, but implied in these orders, would appear to be the assumption that, if a potentially successful Chinese intervention were to be set in motion, it would be recognized in time to allow MacArthur to withdraw gracefully.

In the event, this was not the case. Following initial contact with UN forces at the end of October and the beginning of November, the Chinese forces disengaged on November 8. This reduced the sense of crisis, thereby making Washington less inclined to restrain MacArthur's advance northward or to question his risky decision to divide his forces as they reached the Yalu. MacArthur began his "final" offensive on November 24, which ended in disaster when Chinese forces intervened massively over the next several days.

The mid-November disengagement, and the generally stealthy way in which the Chinese introduced their forces into Korea, has seemed puzzling to American observers who believed that the Chinese wished, or should have wished, to deter U.S. troops from attempting to occupy all of North Korea. As viewed by Thomas Schelling,

> It is not easy to explain why the Chinese entered North Korea so secretly and so suddenly. Had they wanted to stop the United Nations at the level, say, of Pyongyang, to protect their own border and territory, a conspicuous early entry in force might have found the UN Command content with its accomplishments and in no mood to fight a second war, against Chinese armies, for the remainder of

---

[5]This instruction would have been given in early October.

Korea. They chose instead to launch a surprise attack, with stunning tactical advantages *but no prospect of deterrence.* (Schelling, 1966, p. 55; emphasis added.)

Of course, this puzzle disappears if one assumes that the Chinese were no longer interested in deterrence but wished instead to maximize the probability that their intervention would succeed in driving the UN forces off the Korean peninsula. As Christensen's recent work has shown, the key determinant of the Chinese decision to intervene was the crossing by the UN forces of the 38th parallel. Once that happened, Mao was determined to attack in the hope of pushing the United States off the peninsula and avoiding a situation in which the basing of U.S. troops in both Korea and Taiwan would raise the specter of a "two front" attack on China. Thus, based on the contemporaneous Chinese record, it appears that the internal U.S. debate about whether to stop at the "narrow neck" of Korea or go all the way to the Yalu was beside the point. Similarly, U.S. attempts to reassure China that it would neither conduct military activities on the other side of the Yalu nor interfere with Chinese hydroelectric plants on it were similarly irrelevant. (See Whiting, 1960, pp. 151–152.)

If Christensen is right,[6] there was no Chinese attempt to deter the United States from advancing all the way to the Yalu and hence no second deterrence "failure." Having decided to intervene, the Chinese interest lay in making their initial attack as successful as possible. The key requirements for this were, first, American overextension and overconfidence and, second, surprise.

---

[6]Whiting (1960), p. 117, takes a similar view, although he also attributes to the Chinese leadership a desire "to maintain flexibility in case there were a softening of U.S. policy." Whiting describes the other Chinese motives as follows:

> Once the Chinese had ordered their units into action, it was necessary to preserve tactical surprise, as far as this was possible after the warnings of the political phase. It was also desirable, no doubt, to conceal military movements so as to reduce the likelihood of a United States counterblow in the deployment stage. . . .

According to Christensen's analysis, the Chinese did not see any prospect of such an occurrence. In any case, Whiting (1960), p. 114, agrees that

> [t]he timing and nature of the Chinese Communist reaction [to Soviet attempts at the UN to prevent U.S. troops from crossing the 38th parallel] bear out the hypothesis that the crossing of the thirty-eighth parallel was the final contingency determining Peking's entry into the war.

General MacArthur provided the first ingredient in full measure. According to President Truman's account of his Wake Island meeting with MacArthur on October 15,

> He [MacArthur] thought, he said, that there was very little chance that they [the Chinese] would come in. At the most they might be able to get fifty or sixty thousand men into Korea, but, since they had no air force, "if the Chinese tried to get down to Pyongyang, there would be the greatest slaughter." (Truman, 1956, p. 366.)

This is some evidence that the Chinese were aware of his overconfidence and took steps (such as releasing the Americans captured in the first skirmishes) to encourage this misestimate:

> On November 18, 1950, one week before MacArthur's offensive, Mao sent a telegram to [Marshal] Peng [Dehuai] celebrating the American misperception of China's troop strength. Mao knew that MacArthur falsely believed Chinese forces in Korea to consist of only 60,000 or 70,000 troops, when actually there were at least 260,000. Mao told Peng that this was to China's advantage and would assist Chinese forces in destroying "tens of thousands" of enemy troops. In the same telegram, Mao instructed Peng to release prisoners of war.[7]

Marshall Peng later claimed that the release of UN prisoners was designed to encourage MacArthur's further advance northward. (Christensen, 1996, p. 171.) According to Peng,

> First, though we achieved success in the first offensive operation, the enemy's main force remained intact. With the main body of the CPV [Chinese People's Volunteers] unexposed, it was expected that the enemy would continue to stage an offensive. Second, the enemy had boasted the ability of its air force to cut off our communication and food supply. This gave us an opportunity to deceive the enemy about our intention. By releasing some POWs, we could give the enemy the impression that we are in short supply and are retreating. Thirdly, the enemy is equipped with air and tank cover,

---

[7]Christensen (1996), p. 171, citing "Telegram to Peng Dehuai and Others concerning the Release of Prisoners of War," November 18, 1950, *Jianguo Yilai Mao Zedong Wengao*, Vol. 1, p. 672.

so it would be difficult for us to wipe out the retreating enemy on foot.[8]

The result was that the Chinese achieved tactical surprise and an overwhelming victory against the very badly positioned U.S. forces.[9] The Chinese attack illustrates the doctrine of the classic Chinese strategist, Sun Zi (Ch.1, Vs. 17–18, 23, 26–27):

All warfare is based on deception.

Therefore, when capable, feign incapacity; when active, inactivity.
. . .

Pretend inferiority and encourage his arrogance. . . .

Attack where he is unprepared; sally out when he does not expect you.

These are the strategist's keys to victory. It is not possible to discuss them beforehand.

As Schelling notes, this approach to warfare may produce surprise, but not deterrence.

U.S. Concludes an Alliance with Taiwan (1954–1955)[10]

On September 3, 1954, the Chinese PLA began an artillery bombardment of Republic of China (ROC)–held Jinmen island. The U.S. response included the alerting of the Pacific Fleet and the eventual signing, on December 5, of a mutual defense treaty with Taiwan. On January 19, 1955, PRC forces occupied the Yijiangshan Islands, which lie along the Chinese coast several hundred miles north of Taiwan, on the outskirts of the Dachen island group. Soon after, the ROC withdrew from the rest of the Dachens. The Chinese shelling of Jinmen island continued into the spring of 1955.

---

[8]Hao and Zhai (1990), pp. 113–114, citing Yao Xu, *From Yalu River to Panmunjon* (Beijing: People's Press, 1985), pp. 39–40.

[9]As noted, this interpretation relies heavily on Christensen (1996). An alternative interpretation would be that the initial intervention was truly tentative in nature; only when it achieved success did the Chinese decide to intervene in a major way and seek to inflict a significant defeat on the U.S./UN forces.

[10]This account draws heavily on Zhang (1992), pp. 189–224.

The origins of the Taiwan Strait crisis of 1954–1955 may be sought in China's attempt, following the end of the Korean War, to remove what it saw as the threat to itself arising from U.S. military ties to the KMT government in Taiwan. On July 23, 1954, as Premier Zhou Enlai was returning from the Geneva conference on Indochina, Chairman Mao Zedong sent him the following message:

> In order to break up the collaboration between the United States and Chiang Kai-shek, and keep them from joining together militarily and politically, we must announce to our country and to the world the slogan of liberating Taiwan. It was improper of us not to raise this slogan in a timely manner after the cease-fire in Korea. If we were to continue dragging our heels now, we would be making a serious political mistake. (Zhang, 1992, p. 193.[11])

In essence, China attributed to the United States a "three front" strategy: The United States sought to exert military pressure on China from Korea, Vietnam, and Taiwan. By mid-1954, the first two "fronts" had been dealt with. What remained was to try to do something about the potential third "front." (Zhang, 1992, p. 189.) In addition, China may have feared that a formal U.S.-Taiwan alliance was an obvious next step following the formation of the Southeast Asia Treaty Organization (SEATO) and the signing of a mutual defense treaty with South Korea.[12]

Mao's concerns were in line with the advice of Sun Zi (Ch. 3, Vs. 4–7):

> Thus, what is of supreme importance in war is to attack the enemy's strategy.

> Next best is to disrupt his alliances.

> The next best is to attack his army.

> The worst policy is to attack cities. Attack cities only when there is no alternative.

---

[11]Zhang cites an unpublished paper by He Di, a member of the Institute of American Studies, Chinese Academy of Social Sciences. See also He (1990), pp. 222–245.

[12]This is the interpretation put forward by He Di (1990), pp. 224–225:

> With the signing both of a mutual defence treaty with South Korea and the protocol creating the Southeast Asia Treaty Organization the U.S. government entered into negotiations with the Kuomintang to form a mutual defense treaty—the last link in the ring of encirclement of China.

Mao thus sought to disrupt what he took to be the strategy and alliances of the United States.   In fact, both President Eisenhower and Secretary of State Dulles had been reluctant to conclude a mutual security treaty with Taiwan.   Eisenhower thought that such a treaty would be "too big a commitment of U.S. prestige and forces."[13] In any case, there was no enthusiasm for any guarantee that would extend to the offshore islands of Jinmen and Mazu, which were seen as essentially indefensible.   Furthermore, the administration believed that public and allied support for military action in defense of the offshore islands would be hard to obtain.

Nevertheless, U.S. policy shifted toward a treaty with Taiwan, which was concluded on December 5.   A key question was whether the U.S. commitment would extend to the offshore islands; this was left ambiguous in the treaty.   The subsequent Formosa Resolution, passed by Congress on January 28, 1955, took a step in the direction of extending the commitment: It authorized the president to deploy armed forces to protect the offshore islands if he judged that an attack on them was part of an attack on Taiwan.[14]

Following the seizure of the Dachen islands, the Eisenhower administration's fears concerning Chinese intentions with respect to Jinmen and Mazu led to an attempt to threaten the use of nuclear weapons as a deterrent.[15]   Whether for this reason or because the Chinese leadership saw no more advantage in prolonging the crisis, China expressed, in April 1955, an interest in reducing tension in the area.

Although a Chinese scholar has claimed that the crisis "advance[d] Chinese foreign policy interests in several ways,"[16] Christensen's

---

[13]Dulles papers, Conference with the President, May 23, 1954, White House memorandum series, Box 1, Eisenhower Library, cited in Zhang (1992), p. 204.

[14]Hinton (1966), p. 262, suggests that this proviso was insignificant, since Chinese rhetoric always spoke in terms of "liberating" Taiwan.

[15]This point is dealt with in Chapter Three in connection with the discussion of U.S. deterrence efforts with respect to the offshore islands.

[16]He (1990), pp. 230–231, who cites the following gains achieved by China from the crisis:

> First, by opening up a new channel [the Sino-U.S. ambassadorial talks in Warsaw] for dealing directly with the United States, the crisis led to the creation of an important new diplomatic venue for PRC participation in world affairs. Second, the crisis provided Chinese leaders with valuable experience in the design and execution of limited

evaluation of the incident neatly sums up the deterrence failure with respect to the principal objective, as described in the Mao-Zhou message cited above:

> The motivations of Mao's 1954 attack on the offshore islands are fairly clear and have been explored in detail both in the United States and in China: Mao hoped that by attacking in the straits he could dissuade the United States from including Taiwan in new multilateral defense arrangements in Southeast Asia (specifically, SEATO, the Southeast Asia Treaty Organization). The attack was essentially a test of American resolve toward the defense of Taiwan. Mao was warning that any nation signing a defense pact with Taiwan ran the risk of war with Beijing. Mao's attempt backfired. If anything, the attack caused Eisenhower and Dulles to make a clearer and earlier commitment to Taiwan's security than they otherwise would have preferred. (Christensen, 1996, p. 195.)

India Conducts Its "Forward Policy" in Aksai Chin and Eastern Tibet (1959–1962)[17]

Conflicting Indian and Chinese border claims, and Indian insistence on establishing border posts in disputed areas (India's "forward policy"), led to fighting between the two countries in 1962. The border dispute centered on two areas: In the west, India claimed, but did not control, the Aksai Chin, a plateau adjacent to the Indian-held part of Kashmir and lying between Tibet and Xinjiang. This area has strategic significance for China because an important road from Xinjiang to Tibet passes through it. In the east, China claimed, but did not control, a strip of territory south of the McMahon Line dividing the northeastern Indian state of Assam from Tibet (between Bhutan and Burma).[18] Generally speaking, the McMahon Line runs

---

acts of war with bold acts of political initiative .... The Jinmen crisis also comprised an important watershed in China's search for strategic leverage: the bombardment of Jinmen demonstrated—at relatively low risk—China's determination to reunify the country, which served to increase the urgency of Sino-American contacts and led to the elevation of the Geneva talks to the ambassadorial level, ... Finally, the Jinmen bombardment could be used to exacerbate rifts with the opposition camp. The Jinmen experience thus provided an important lesson in the pursuit of political interest through military means—a lesson the Chinese leaders were to apply in later years.

[17]This section draws heavily on Maxwell (1970) and Liu (1994), Ch. 2.

[18]The McMahon Line was negotiated in 1914 between British officials in India and Tibetan authorities; China claimed that it never recognized as valid any bilateral

along the crest of the Assam Himalayas, while the Chinese claim line runs along the lower edge of the foothills.[19] As part of the forward policy, the Indians had established outposts in disputed areas in the west and along the McMahon Line; in some cases, the outposts were north of the line as it had been originally drawn.[20]

On October 20, 1962, the Chinese launched major attacks, which succeeded immediately, in both the eastern and western sectors; in the former, they pushed the Indians out of the territory north of the McMahon Line (as the Chinese understood it); in the latter, they destroyed most of the Indian outposts in the disputed territory.

After a short pause, the Chinese renewed their attacks in mid-November (in one case, an Indian offensive action planned for November 14 failed, leading to a successful counterattack); by November 20, no organized Indian units remained in the entire disputed territory south of the McMahon Line. The rout of the Indian troops left the Chinese poised to strike southward into the Indian state of Assam. The Chinese military victory was complete. At this point, the Chinese announced a unilateral cease-fire and withdrew to positions 20 km behind the line of actual control of November 7, 1959. They "reserved the right to strike back" if the Indian armed forces did not remain 20 km back of the line of actual control as well. The Indian army ordered its soldiers to observe the cease-fire, but, at the political level, India remained noncommittal (Maxwell, 1970, pp. 417–421); the Indians abandoned their forward policy, and the conflict abated.

Given the one-sided result of the fighting, the Chinese failure, prior to October 1962, to deter India from pursuing its forward policy (or, after the first clashes in October 1962, to compel India to abandon it) is puzzling. In the western sector (the Aksai Chin plateau), the Indians realized that their own forces were outnumbered by the Chinese; in addition, their logistics capabilities were so poor that

---

British-Tibetan agreement. The "diplomatic hugger-mugger" by means of which this was achieved is described in Maxwell (1970), pp. 47–52.

[19]There was also a much-less-important third area where overlapping claims existed (the "middle sector"), between Aksai Chin and Nepal.

[20]The Indians made these adjustments to the line unilaterally, to have it follow topographic features, such as ridge lines.

most posts had to be supplied by airdrop, which meant that they had to stick to the valley floors, while the Chinese could take up dominating positions on higher ground. All in all, the forward policy was extremely risky for the troops involved, as Indian Prime Minister Nehru admitted to the parliament:

> We built a kind of rampart on this part of Ladakh [the Aksai Chin] and put up numerous military posts, small ones and big ones. . . . It is true that these posts are in constant danger of attack with larger numbers. Well, it does not matter. We have taken the risk and we have moved forward, and we have effectively stopped their further forward march. . . . If [the Chinese] want to they can overwhelm some of our military posts. That does not mean we are defeated. We shall face them with much greater problems and face them much more stoutly.[21]

Despite this recognition of the inherent risk involved, the basic belief that the Chinese would not attack the weaker Indian positions held firm. Similarly, in the east, the Indians suffered significant disadvantages in terms of logistics and mobility, although it is less clear how aware they were of them.[22] At various points, the Indian political leadership asserted that conditions in the east were militarily favorable to them, although the military leadership understood the precarious situation of some of its advanced positions.

The key point, however, is that the Indians were convinced that the Chinese would not attack. Throughout the period, even after their initial defeats in October, the Indians did not believe that the Chinese would launch a massive attack on them.

During the months before the conflict, China issued a series of warnings, both diplomatic notes and public statements, attacking the Indian forward policy. Nevertheless, the tone was often relatively restrained. For example, the Chinese, in a diplomatic note dated June 2, 1962, after accusing the Indians of seeking "to provoke bloody conflicts, occupy China's territory and change the status quo of the

---

[21]Maxwell (1970), p. 254, quoting a Nehru speech to parliament in August 1962.

[22]For example, at a key point along the McMahon Line, the Indian positions were five days' march from the nearest road, while the Chinese, based on the Tibetan plateau, had an all-weather road that extended to within three hours' march of their position.

boundary regardless of consequences," nevertheless concluded as follows:

> The Chinese government consistently stands for a peaceful settlement of the Sino-Indian boundary question through negotiations. Even now when the Sino-Indian border situation has become so tense owing to Indian aggression and provocation, the door for negotiations is still open so far as the Chinese side concerned [sic]. However, China will never submit before any threat of force.[23]

Other notes warned that "India will be held responsible for all the consequences" arising from its intrusions; but this was coupled with an assertion that the Chinese government strove "to avoid clashes with intruding Indian troops."[24] The Indians may have regarded this verbal posture as not particularly threatening; it seemed to imply only that the Chinese would fight back if attacked. Thus, the Indians may have believed that, as long as their forces did not initiate conflict with the Chinese, the forward policy could continue as a form of shadow boxing, with each side maneuvering its patrols to gain positional advantage, but without actually coming to blows.

Perhaps more importantly, Chinese behavior was restrained as well. The Indian forward policy inevitably led to situations in which units of the two armies confronted each other in close proximity. In two instances, in May and July 1962, Chinese troops adopted threatening postures with respect to newly implanted Indian posts; in the latter case, they surrounded an Indian post and blocked an attempt to resupply it by land, forcing it to rely on airdrops. Nevertheless, in both cases, the Chinese did not follow through on their implicit threats and refrained from actually attacking the posts. This served to confirm, for the Indians, the wisdom of the forward policy: If the Indians were resolute, the Chinese would not use force to interfere with their strategy of creating a network of new posts. (Maxwell, 1970, p. 239.)

China's pause between its initial victories in October and its all-out offensive in mid-November may also have served to give the Indians an unfounded confidence in their assessment of Chinese inten-

---

[23]New China News Agency–English, Peking, June 9, 1962.

[24]Chinese government memorandum of July 8, 1962 handed to the Indian chargé d'affaires in Beijing, New China News Agency–English, Beijing, July 8, 1962.

tions.[25] During the "pause," Chinese troops infiltrated India's Northeast Frontier Agency by means of a side trail, outflanking the new Indian defensive position established after the initial reverse. But if, for the Chinese, the pause presented the opportunity to regroup and infiltrate troops behind the main Indian positions, the Indians appeared to interpret it as a sign that the Chinese would not, or could not, pursue their attack any further. At the same time, the Indians held an exaggerated view of their own strength, believing that they were now able to resist any Chinese attack.[26]

Underlying this Indian confidence was a perception of Chinese weakness, caused in part by the failure of the Great Leap Forward, which eventuated in the great famine of the early 1960s. This man-made disaster, compounded by difficult weather conditions, is estimated to have cost the lives of 30 million Chinese. No doubt, the Indian leadership believed that a weakened China was in no position to risk war, especially with a country that was, in global geopolitical terms, generally friendly.[27]

On the other hand, the Chinese leadership probably drew a different conclusion from their domestic troubles, i.e., that India was deliberately trying to take advantage of them, and thus that its forward policy was even more dangerous than might appear on the surface. In Allen Whiting's view,

> Ironically New Delhi and Peking shared a common assessment of China's weakness; however, where Indian logic argued this would prevent the PLA from fighting, Chinese logic saw it as compelling strong action. New Delhi and Peking also agreed on Indian weakness, but here New Delhi assumed this obviously made its behavior harmless, although Peking saw it as necessitating some larger, hidden design, aided and abetted from outside. (Whiting, 1975, p. 169.)

---

[25]This is similar to what occurred in Korea in November 1950.

[26]For example, on November 12, Home Minister Lal Bahadur Shastri claimed that "India was now strong enough to repulse the Chinese attackers and was building its military might to drive the invaders from Indian soil." (Maxwell, 1970, p. 387.)

[27]For example, India had always been a major supporter of PRC membership in the United Nations; in the mid-1950s, Sino-Indian friendship became a major foreign policy principle for both governments.

Although India thought it was only vindicating its territorial claims, China may have interpreted its behavior as being part of a more complex and sinister plot. Precisely because India was behaving in such a reckless fashion, China may have suspected that it was merely the spearhead of a much more dangerous anti-Chinese combination, perhaps involving Taiwan, the United States, and the Soviet Union (which, except at the height of the Cuban missile crisis, had tended to "tilt" toward India). As Whiting summarizes,

> Paradoxically, while India maintained a benign misconception, China held a malevolent one, firm in the belief that persistent advances behind PLA outposts represented at least New Delhi's aggressive design and most probably collusion with Moscow or Washington or both. (Whiting, 1975, p. 168.)

From this perspective, it is possible to deduce a reason China did not attempt to deter India in a more explicit and threatening fashion. Conceiving of Indian policy as being more aggressive, purposeful, and settled than it in fact was, China would have concluded that threats could not be an adequate deterrent; surely India would have already discounted them. Only forceful action, producing a psychological shock for which India was not prepared, could cause the Indian leadership to change course.

Vietnam Invades Cambodia (1978–1979)[28]

Traditional tensions between China and Vietnam, which were suppressed during the Vietnam War, began to reemerge in 1974 as the North Vietnamese victory approached. That January, the Chinese seized the South Vietnamese–held islands of the Paracel (Xisha) group, which were claimed by China and both Vietnamese governments. The timing was propitious: The United States was disengaging from the region (and in any case was more concerned about pursuing its *rapprochement* with China); Saigon had bigger problems to deal with; and Hanoi was not yet in a position to challenge China, from whom it was still receiving some support for its war effort.

---

[28]This section draws heavily on Ross (1988).

In addition, there were incidents on the contested land border between China and North Vietnam. China proposed negotiations on this issue in spring 1975, as the war was coming to a close, but North Vietnam rejected the offer, reportedly replying that it "had a lot of work to do in view of the developments in the liberation of South Vietnam." (Ross, 1988, p. 37.)

After Hanoi's victory in 1975, the key issue in Chinese-Vietnamese relations became the nature and extent of the tie between Vietnam and the Soviet Union; from China's perspective, Vietnam's desire to be a "regional hegemon" in Indochina led to a relationship with the Soviet Union that was too close for China's comfort. By 1978, additional issues between Vietnam and China included, aside from the border, Vietnamese mistreatment of Chinese nationals in Vietnam (the Chinese were disproportionately hurt by the suppression of the private economy in South Vietnam) and the impending Vietnamese invasion of Cambodia and overthrow of the (Chinese-supported) Khmer Rouge.

The Vietnamese concluded a "Friendship and Cooperation Treaty" with the Soviet Union on November 3, 1978, and invaded Cambodia on December 25, 1978. Given the subsequent Chinese reaction— China launched a limited invasion of Vietnam on February 17, 1979—the Vietnamese invasion of Cambodia could be seen as a failure of Chinese deterrence. The Chinese invasion similarly "failed" to compel Vietnam's withdrawal from Cambodia, which did not occur until years later, after Vietnam's Soviet ties had become irrelevant.[29]

The Chinese issued a series of strong warning statements to Vietnam in 1978. The warnings, however, tended to be somewhat ambiguous about exactly what action the Chinese were trying to deter, assuming

---

[29]As noted above, it is often unclear, in a case of this sort, whether the Chinese leadership believed itself to be engaged in deterrence, i.e., whether it took the steps it did with the expectation that the target of those steps (in this case, Vietnam) might, as a result, refrain from doing something China wished it not to do (in this case, invade Cambodia). It is equally possible that the warnings related in the text were designed primarily to prepare domestic and foreign opinion for an intended Chinese invasion of Vietnam and that the Chinese leadership had no real expectation that it could deter Vietnam. Pollack (1984), p. 37, takes the latter view, stressing that "[t]he Chinese apparently regarded a forceful response to the Vietnamese invasion of Kampuchea as an immediate necessity."

that was their purpose. For example, on November 10, 1978, the *People's Daily* carried an editorial, which read in part:

> Under the support and direction of the Soviet Union, [the leaders in Hanoi] have made incessant provocations along the Sino-Vietnamese border and nibbled away at Chinese territory following their wanton anti-China and anti-Chinese activities over the Chinese nationals question. . . .
>
> The Vietnamese authorities have gone farther and farther down the anti-China road by escalating from persecution of and ostracism against Chinese residents to the creation of incidents against the Sino-Vietnamese border. . . .
>
> Both the Soviet Union and Vietnam regard China as the biggest hindrance to the implementation of their designs of hegemonism and regional hegemonism. . . . It is by no means accidental that the Vietnamese authorities engineered the incident on the Sino-Vietnamese border on the eve of their intensified aggression on Kampuchea and conclusion of a military alliance with the Soviet Union. . . .
>
> We sternly warn the Vietnamese authorities: Draw back your criminal hand stretched to Chinese territory and stop the provocation and intrusion along the Chinese-Vietnamese border.
>
> The Vietnamese authorities had better not turn a deaf ear to China's warning.[30]

Thus, the statement explicitly warned Vietnam only against further border incidents; to the extent that it conveyed a deterrent threat, it would appear the Vietnamese actions to be deterred were the "provocation(s) and intrusion(s) along the Chinese-Vietnamese border." However, the statement linked this unacceptable border activity (by means of the well-known locution "it is by no means accidental that") to Vietnam's treaty with the Soviet Union and its intervention in Cambodia, which were presumably China's real concerns.

Months later, and only a week before the Chinese invasion of Vietnam, China's rhetorical emphasis remained on the border dis-

---

[30]New China News Agency–English, Peking, 2010 GMT November 9, 1978, in FBIS-CHI, November 13, 1978, pp. A8–A9.

pute. For example, on February 10, 1979, the Ministry of Foreign Affairs delivered a note to Vietnam, which listed a series of border incidents and then concluded:

> The Chinese Government hereby expresses its utmost indignation at the above new crimes committed by the Vietnamese authorities. . . . The Vietnamese authorities must stop their military provocations against China; otherwise they must be held responsible for all the consequences arising therefrom.[31]

Not only did China's statements not specify the actions with which it was primarily concerned, but China does not appear to have made any attempt to escalate the vehemence of its warnings so as to indicate the imminence of its invasion. (Segal, 1985, p. 213.) Indeed, it appears that, despite its warnings, China was able to achieve some measure of tactical surprise.[32]

However, the major reason Vietnam was able to shrug off these warnings was probably that it was confident that its own strength, backed by the support of the Soviet Union, if required, would be sufficient to handle any Chinese military challenge. As discussed in Chapter Three, China was quite aware of the limitations the Vietnamese-Soviet alliance imposed on its military freedom of action. To succeed, China had to achieve a major victory quickly, before Soviet military capabilities could be brought to bear; only by means of such a psychological shock could China hope to secure a political change in Hanoi. This China was unable to do.

SUCCESSES

As opposed to these four more or less clear examples of cases in which Chinese adversaries took steps China had wished to prevent, Chinese deterrence successes are harder to affirm with certainty. This section discusses three possible candidates:

---

[31]Perhaps because this was an official government note, it did not mention the other sources of Chinese concerns; in particular, it was silent on the Vietnamese invasion of Cambodia, which had already succeeded in toppling the Khmer Rouge regime. Xinhua—English, Beijing, 1639 GMT February 10, 1979 in FBIS-CHI, February 12, 1979, pp. A6–A7.

[32]The evidence for this is that most of the Vietnamese leadership was away from Hanoi on February 17, when the actual invasion began. (Segal, 1985, p. 215.)

- U.S. ground troops stay out of North Vietnam.

- Soviets do not attack China (1968–1969).

- Taiwan scales back campaign to bolster diplomatic status (1996).

In each case, one could question whether the label "success" is justified: One could argue that the first case involved U.S. self-deterrence and that the second involved a situation in which the Soviet Union did not intend to attack China in any case; and the third had an ambiguous result in which China did not get much of what it wanted.

U.S. Ground Troops Stay Out of North Vietnam

The record is fairly clear that U.S. decisionmakers were very aware of the Korean War experience as they planned U.S. strategy at the beginning of the Vietnam War. As one observer has noted, if one set of lessons from Korea dealt with the importance of making clear commitments and countering aggression, another lesson had to do with the costs of provoking China in the process:

> That Lyndon Johnson and his civilian advisors were mindful of China is not controversial. In fact, one of the things about which there is a strong consensus among Johnson's former military and civilian advisors is that this last lesson of Korea, the specter of Chinese intervention, constrained American strategy in Vietnam decisively. If the other five lessons of Korea suggested that the United States ought to intervene and win in Vietnam, this sixth lesson reminded the policymakers of the necessity of avoiding another war with China. . . . Looked at this way, the stakes of avoiding war with China were as high, if not higher than, the stakes in Vietnam. (Khong, 1992, pp. 136–137.)

If this is so, Chinese intervention in the Korean War served a deterrent purpose in Vietnam; it helped restrain the United States from sending ground troops into North Vietnam and, especially in the early part of the war, helped maintain a sanctuary from aerial attack in the areas of North Vietnam closest to China. In general, it may even be said that the United States had "overlearned" the lesson of the Korean War and that, initially at least, the United States deterred itself from steps it could have taken without provoking Chinese intervention. According to Secretary of State Dean Rusk, discussing the early decisionmaking process in 1963 and 1964,

> The bombing was also related to the question as to whether the war would expand and whether Red China could come in. If anyone had asked me in 1963 whether we could have half a million men in South Viet Nam and bomb everything in the North right up to the Chinese border without bringing in Red China, I would have been hard put to say that you could.[33]

Indeed, none of the options considered in 1964–1965 involved sending U.S. troops into North Vietnam. Yet, despite an intelligence assessment of early 1965 that only a ground invasion of North Vietnam or the toppling of the Hanoi regime would trigger Chinese intervention (Johnson, 1971, p. 125), Johnson decided against the more aggressive options under consideration—"bring[ing] the enemy to his knees by using our Strategic Air Command" and "call[ing] up the reserves and increas[ing] the draft" and "go[ing] on a war footing," both to support a major land war and to signal resolve—for fear of provoking a larger war:

> I believed that we should do what was necessary to resist aggression but that we should not be provoked into a major war. We would get the required appropriation in the new budget, and we would not boast about what we were doing. We would not make threatening noises to the Chinese or the Russians by calling up reserves in large numbers. (Johnson, 1971, p. 149.)

Thus, one may say that Chinese intervention in Korea exercised, more than a decade later, a deterrent effect on the United States with respect to its actions in Vietnam. While this may not be an example of deterrence according to the criteria set out by international relations theorists (since there was little contemporaneous Chinese action directed toward deterring the United States), it is worth noting nonetheless.

---

[33]Transcript, Dean Rusk Oral History Interview, p. 24, as cited in Khong (1992), p. 143.

Soviets Do Not Attack China (1969)[34]

The Soviet invasion of Czechoslovakia in August 1968 and the promulgation of the "Brezhnev Doctrine," which justified it in terms of the limited sovereignty of socialist states (with respect to the larger socialist community), raised the temperature of the Sino-Soviet dispute, which had up to that point centered on ideological differences. The Chinese had indeed already raised the question of the 19th century "unequal treaties" between Tsarist Russia and Imperial China, by means of which Russia gained large tracts of land in what became the Russian Far East; however, the 1968 invasion also introduced a security aspect to the dispute.

In September 1968, the Chinese complained about intrusions of Russian aircraft into their airspace during the previous month (including, in particular, the period of Russian military operations in Czechoslovakia). The Chinese broadened this complaint into a campaign to indict the Soviet Union for "social imperialism," the criminal nature of which was portrayed as being equal in gravity to the "imperialism" of the United States. Primary targets for this campaign were the communist parties of the world, especially the ruling parties of China's neighbors, North Korea and North Vietnam. Especially with respect to the latter, which was heavily dependent on Soviet military supplies, this campaign was not successful.

On March 2, 1969, after a period of mounting tensions, a major firefight occurred on Zhenbao (Damanskiy) Island in the Ussuri River, a piece of real estate contested between China and the Soviet Union. Although it lay on the Chinese side of the main shipping channel or *thalweg*, the Soviets claimed it on the grounds that, by treaty, the border ran along the Chinese shore.[35]

The clash appears to have resulted from a Chinese initiative, i.e., its decision to patrol disputed territory aggressively that had only seen Chinese civilian activity before. Chinese tactics—the use of a lead patrol to draw out Soviet border guards and a subsequent ambush by

---

[34]This section draws heavily on Wich (1980) and Segal (1985), Ch. 10.

[35]This border dispute resembled that with the Indians concerning the McMahon Line: Although *in principle* the Chinese rejected the existing boundaries altogether, since they considered the treaties that established the borders to be invalid, they accepted the borders *in practice*. The actual fighting resulted from differences concerning the detailed demarcation of the boundary lines contained in the treaties.

other Chinese forces—seemed designed to ensure that casualties would be higher than in previous incidents.[36]   Most tellingly, the Chinese launched a major propaganda campaign on the basis of the incident, while Soviet press coverage was more low key and reactive. (Segal, 1985, p. 194, fn. 6.)

The Soviets responded by bringing superior firepower to bear in the course of a second incident on the same island on March 15:

> The new pattern of differentiated reaction by the two sides—with the Soviets being the ones this time [March 15] to make a big fuss over the event—gave further confirmation to the interpretation that the first clash resulted from a Chinese challenge to the existing rules of the game along the border, but that the second one resulted mainly from a Soviet determination to demonstrate the dangers of escalation inherent in the Chinese use of arms in border challenges. (Wich, 1980, p. 113.)

Despite this Soviet show of force, the Chinese resisted Soviet efforts to convene talks on the border problem, going so far as to refuse a phone call from Soviet Premier Kosygin on March 21.[37]   It was not until September 11 that the Chinese consented to receive Kosygin, who had been in Hanoi to attend Ho Chi Minh's funeral. That Ho's "testament" called for Sino-Soviet reconciliation may have made it easier for the Chinese to take this step. Even so, their "invitation" reached Kosygin only after he was already in Soviet Central Asia on his return trip to Moscow, forcing him to double back to Beijing. Whether this humiliation was deliberate, or resulted from slow Chinese decisionmaking, is not clear.

Whether or not the Soviets ever intended to apply the Brezhnev Doctrine to China, the Chinese behavior at the border may have been designed, at least in part, to serve notice that China would be no Czechoslovakia. As noted above,[38] the Soviet Union did make some vague nuclear threats against China (but these occurred after the initial border incidents and were probably designed to force China to

---

[36]For a detailed description of this clash and of the subsequent one on March 15, see Robinson (1970), pp. 33–40.

[37]Chinese Defense Minister Lin Biao announced this at the Ninth Congress of the Chinese Communist Party in April 1969, evidently to humiliate the Soviet Union.

[38]See the discussion of the Soviet deterrence of China in Chapter Three.

the bargaining table). After the initial border incidents in March, the Chinese were not so much trying to deter a Soviet attack as to resist the Soviet efforts to compel them to come to the bargaining table; in this, the Chinese were ultimately unsuccessful, and talks opened between the two countries on October 20, 1969. To the extent that the Soviets were deterred from attacking China, credit should probably go to the People's War doctrine, which promised a difficult, long-drawn-out struggle, and to the incalculability of the consequences of a Soviet nuclear strike.

Taiwan Scales Back Campaign to Bolster Diplomatic Status (1996)[39]

During March 1996, China conducted a series of military exercises that included missile tests to two maritime areas adjacent to Taiwan's major ports; live fire exercises by air; land and naval forces in an exercise area off the coast of Fujian province and immediately south of the Taiwan Strait; and an amphibious, helicopter, and parachute assault on an island in the northern end of the Taiwan Strait. (Garver, 1997, pp. 100–107.) These exercises ran from March 8 to 25, thus coinciding with Taiwan's first democratic presidential election on March 23 and the final weeks of the political campaign.

The exercises appeared designed to affect the election and bolster the chances of the New Party, a breakaway group from the KMT, which had remained loyal to Chiang Kai-shek's policy with respect to the ROC's claim to be the legitimate government of all of China. By contrast, Lee Teng-hui, the incumbent president and the KMT candidate for reelection, had deviated from that policy by adopting a "pragmatic diplomacy" that recognized the existence of two separate Chinese governments (the PRC and the ROC), one of which ruled the mainland and the other, Taiwan. On the basis of this approach, he sought to expand his government's "international space" by, among other things, seeking membership in various international organizations, including the United Nations. Thus,

> In September 1993 Taipei announced its new goal of joining the [UN] General Assembly as the "Republic of China" under the

---

[39]This section draws heavily on Garver (1997).

> "divided state" formula that had allowed the two Germanys and the two Koreas to join. . . .
>
> In preparation for its [1995 UN] bid, Taipei said that it might donate $1 billion to the UN if it were allowed to become a member. This time Taiwan gained the support of twenty-nine countries. (Garver, 1997, p. 31.)

Another target of the exercises was U.S. policy. In the 1992–1995 period, several U.S. actions regarding Taiwan—notably the F-16 sales President Bush announced during the 1992 election campaign and the decision in May 1995 to allow President Lee Teng-hui of Taiwan to make a "private visit" to the United States—had disturbed Chinese leaders and raised the specter of a secret U.S. plan to "contain" China by supporting a Taiwanese bid for independence. In any case, the U.S. actions could encourage Taiwanese independence forces.

The 1996 exercise followed a less threatening series of missile tests the previous year, which, arguably, had succeeded in influencing the Taiwanese legislative elections held in December 1995. In that election, the KMT had lost seven seats (holding on to 85, a bare majority of the Legislative Yuan), while the New Party tripled its representation to 21. In terms of popular vote, the KMT fell below a majority, winning only 46 percent. The Democratic Progressive Party (DPP), which had been formed in opposition to the KMT, calling for both democracy and independence, gained four seats (to 54); this was much less than the party had expected to win in Taiwan's first fully democratic legislative election.

With respect to the presidential election itself, by contrast, Beijing's muscle-flexing was a failure: Lee Teng-hui was reelected with 54 percent of the vote. China's military pressure probably swung DPP votes toward the KMT, as proindependence voters understood the need for greater unity in response to Chinese pressure. Conversely, in the absence of the crisis, the election would arguably have turned more on domestic issues (such as crime, corruption, and social problems), in which case the two opposition parties might well have denied the KMT a majority.[40]

---

[40]Garver (1997), pp. 152–153, notes that the two opposition parties were prepared to cooperate on domestic issues; but this ended once China's actions made independence versus unification the primary issue of the campaign.

China also failed to produce a major panic on Taiwan that could have caused the elections to be canceled and Taiwan's democratization to be thrown off track. While there was some capital outflow and panic hoarding of food and other items, the overall effect remained minor and insufficient to produce any political consequences. A major reason for this was U.S. deployment of two carrier battle groups as the exercises progressed. These tended to counterbalance the psychological pressure of the exercises with the psychological assurance of U.S. support in case of more serious Chinese military actions.

Despite the immediate failure with respect to the presidential elections itself, the Chinese exercises achieved some of the desired results.[41] Taiwan has, generally speaking, been less aggressive in its pursuit of such forms of international recognition as UN membership. Certainly, the population of Taiwan has been put on notice that open support for independence could lead China to take military action; in the December 1977 local elections, for example, the DPP emphasized local issues rather than independence in its generally successful campaign.

Similarly, U.S. policy turned more toward improving relations with China, leading eventually to Chinese President Jiang Zemin's visit to Washington in 1997 and President Clinton's return visit to China in 1998. It is certainly unlikely that Lee Teng-hui will be granted another visa.

In the long run, China may still pay a price for its actions: Taiwanese public opinion may be more suspicious of China and less willing to accept a "one country, two systems" outcome, while the United States and the other countries in the region may be more wary of growing Chinese military power. However, in the near term, China may well feel that it successfully deterred both Taiwan and the United States from going further down a path that could only lead, sooner or later, to Taiwanese independence.

---

[41]This analysis of gains and losses was completed before Lee Teng-hui, in July 1999, announced that Taiwan would pursue relations with China on a "special state-to-state" basis, i.e., he asserted that the PRC and ROC were separate "states," albeit within one Chinese nation. See Faison (1999).

BIBLIOGRAPHY

"The Adventurist Course of Peking," editorial, *Pravda*, August 28, 1969, in FBIS-SOV, August 28, 1969, pp. A1–A7.

Burles, Mark, and Abram N. Shulsky, *Patterns in China's Use of Force: Evidence from History and Doctrinal Writings*, Santa Monica, Calif.: RAND, MR-1160-AF, 2000.

Christensen, Thomas J., "Threats, Assurances, and the Last Chance for Peace: The Lessons of Mao's Korean War Telegrams," *International Security*, Vol. 17, No. 1, Summer 1992, pp. 122–154.

_____, *Useful Adversaries: Grand Strategy, Domestic Mobilization, and Sino-American Conflict, 1947–1958*, Princeton, N.J.: Princeton University Press, 1996.

Cohen, Warren I., and Akira Iriye, eds., *The Great Powers in East Asia, 1953–1960*, New York: Columbia University Press, 1990.

Deocadiz, Christina V., *Business World* (Internet Version), August 6, 1998, transcribed as "Philippines: [Foreign Affairs Secretary Domingo] Siazon: US to 'Aid' Manila in Event of Spratlys Attack," in FBIS-EAS-98-218.

Eisenhower, Dwight D., *Mandate for Change: 1953–56*, Garden City, N.Y.: Doubleday & Company, Inc., 1963.

Faison, Seth, "Taiwan President Implies His Island Is Sovereign State," *New York Times*, July 13, 1999.

Garver, John W., *Face Off: China, the United States, and Taiwan's Democratization*, Seattle: University of Washington Press, 1997.

Gelman, Harry, *The Soviet Far East Buildup and Soviet Risk-Taking Against China*, Santa Monica, Calif.: RAND, R-2943-AF, August 1982.

George, Alexander L., and Richard Smoke, *Deterrence in American Foreign Policy: Theory and Practice*, New York: Columbia University Press, 1974.

Gilpin, Robert, *War and Change in World Politics*, paperback ed., Cambridge, U.K.: Cambridge University Press, 1983.

Hao Yufan and Zhai Zhihai, "China's Decision to Enter the Korean War," *China Quarterly*, No. 121, March 1990.

Harding, Harry, *A Fragile Relationship: The United States and China Since 1972*, Washington, D.C.: Brookings, 1992.

He Di, "The Evolution of the People's Republic of China's Policy Toward the Offshore Islands," in Warren I. Cohen and Akira Iriye, eds., *The Great Powers in East Asia, 1953–1960*, New York: Columbia University Press, 1990.

Hinton, Harold C., *Communist China in World Politics*, Boston: Houghton Mifflin, 1966.

_____, "Conflict on the Ussuri: A Clash of Nationalism," *Problems of Communism*, January–April 1971.

Holloway, Nigel, "Jolt from the Blue," *Far Eastern Economic Review*, August 3, 1995.

Huth, Paul K., *Extended Deterrence and the Prevention of War*, New Haven, Conn.: Yale University Press, 1988.

Jervis, Robert, "Deterrence Theory Revisited," *World Politics*, Vol. 31, No. 2, January 1979, pp. 289–324.

"Jiang Issues Campus Gag Order on Diaoyu Islands," *Hong Kong Standard*, September 17, 1996, p. 1.

Jiang Zemin, "Continue to Promote the Reunification of the Motherland," 30 January 1995, as reported by Beijing Xinhua in English, 0618 GMT 30 January 95, in FBIS-CHI-95-019.

Johnson, Lyndon B., *The Vantage Point: Perspectives of the Presidency, 1963–69*, New York: Holt, Rinehart and Winston, 1971.

Kahn, Herman, *Thinking About the Unthinkable*, New York: Horizon Press, 1962.

Khalilzad, Zalmay, et al., *The U.S. and a Rising China: Strategic and Military Implications*, Santa Monica, Calif.: RAND, MR-1082-AF, 1999.

Khong, Yuen Foong, *Analogies at War: Korea, Munich, Dien Bien Phu, and the Vietnam Decisions of 1965*, Princeton, N.J.: Princeton University Press, 1992.

Kissinger, Henry, *White House Years*, Boston: Little, Brown and Company, 1979.

Liu, Xuecheng, *The Sino-Indian Border Dispute and Sino-Indian Relations*, Lanham, Md.: University Press of America, 1994.

Maxwell, Neville, *India's China War*, New York: Random House, 1970.

Mirov, A., "The Sinkiang Tragedy," *Literaturnaya Gazeta*, May 7, 1969.

Morgan, Patrick M., *Deterrence: A Conceptual Analysis*, 2nd ed., Beverly Hills, Calif.: Sage Publications, 1983.

Peking New China News Agency in English, editorial, 2010 GMT 9 November 1978, in FBIS-CHI, November 13, 1978, pp. A8–A9.

Pollack, Jonathan D., *The Lessons of Coalition Politics: Sino-American Security Relations*, Santa Monica, Calif.: RAND, R-3133-AF, 1984.

Pomfret, John, "Clinton Restates 'Three Noes' Policy on Taiwan," *Washington Post*, June 30, 1998, p. A12.

Robinson, Thomas W., *The Sino-Soviet Border Dispute: Background, Development, and the March 1969 Clashes*, Santa Monica, Calif.: RAND, RM-6171-PR, 1970.

Ross, Robert S., *The Indochina Tangle: China's Vietnam Policy, 1975–1979*, New York: Columbia University Press, 1988.

Schelling, Thomas C., *Arms and Influence*, New Haven, Conn.: Yale University Press, 1966.

Segal, Gerald, *Defending China*, Oxford: Oxford University Press, 1985.

Snyder, Glenn H., *Deterrence and Defense: Toward a Theory of National Security*, Princeton, N.J.: Princeton University Press, 1961.

Stillion, John, and David T. Orletsky, *Airbase Vulnerability to Conventional Cruise-Missile and Ballistic-Missile Attacks*, Santa Monica, Calif.: RAND, MR-1028-AF, 1999.

Stolper, Thomas E., *China, Taiwan, and the Offshore Islands*, Armonk, N.Y.: M. E. Sharpe, Inc., 1985.

Strong, Anna Louise, "Chinese Strategy in the Taiwan Strait," *New Times* (Moscow), No. 46, November 1958, pp. 8–11.

Sun Zi, *The Art of War*, Samuel B. Griffith, trans., London: Oxford University Press, 1963.

Swaine, Michael D., and Ashley J. Tellis, *Interpreting China's Grand Strategy: Past, Present, and Future*, Santa Monica, Calif.: RAND, MR-1121-AF, 2000.

Taipov, Zunun, "Maoist Outrages on Uigur [sic] Soil," *New Times*, No. 27, July 9, 1969, pp. 11–12.

Thompson, William R., *On Global War*, Columbia: University of South Carolina Press, 1988.

Truman, Harry S., *Memoirs*, Vol. 2: *Years of Trial and Hope*, Garden City, N.Y.: Doubleday, 1956.

Tsou, Tang, *America's Failure in China, 1941–50*, Chicago: University of Chicago Press, 1963.

Tyler, Patrick E., "As China Threatens Taiwan, It Makes Sure U.S. Listens," *New York Times*, January 24, 1996, p. A3.

U.S. Department of Defense, *The United States Security Strategy for the East Asia-Pacific Region: 1998*, Washington, D.C., 1998.

Valencia, Mark J., *China and the South China Sea Disputes*, Adelphi Paper 298, Oxford: Oxford University Press for IISS, 1995.

Wang Jisi, "The Role of the United States as a Global and Pacific Power: A View from China," *The Pacific Review*, Vol. 10, No. 1, 1997, pp. 1–18.

Whiting, Allen S., *China Crosses the Yalu: The Decision to Enter the Korean War*, New York: Macmillan Company, 1960.

_____, *The Chinese Calculus of Deterrence: India and Indochina*, Ann Arbor: University of Michigan Press, 1975.

Wich, Richard, *Sino-Soviet Crisis Politics: A Study of Political Change and Communication*, Cambridge, Mass.: Harvard University Press, 1980.

"X" [George F. Kennan], "The Sources of Soviet Conduct," *Foreign Affairs*, Vol. 25, No. 4, July 1947, pp. 566–582.

Zhang, Shu Guang, *Deterrence and Strategic Culture: Chinese-American Confrontations, 1949–1958*, Ithaca, N.Y.: Cornell University Press, 1992.